Praise for
Take Control of Your Job Search!

"The actionable resources provided in *Take Control of Your Job Search!* will guide anyone looking for a job through the maze of emotions they are experiencing and help them find and land their next job."

> – Ceree Eberly, Global Chair of the Gartner Human Resources Executive Board and former Chief HR Officer at Coca-Cola

"During my 30+ years in the staffing industry, I've seen job candidates experience the full array of emotions. Most often, they are unaware of how their emotions negatively impact their search. *Take Control of Your Job Search!* gives job seekers tools to be more aware of their emotions and practical strategies to take control of their search."

> – Joyce Russell, President, The ADECCO Group US Foundation and Author of *Put a Cherry on Top: Generosity in Life & Leadership*

"Finally! A book that focuses on the underlying emotional intelligence required to land a job in today's market. Herring takes a refreshing and necessary approach to build a key skillset for job seekers not previously addressed by the traditional job search books."

> – Susan Packard, Co-Founder, HGTV, and Author of *New Rules of the Game* and *Fully Human*

i

"As a career coach and Licensed Psychologist, I can confirm that emotions play a part in every human interaction and are central to the job search and hiring processes. *Take Control of Your Career!* highlights an often overlooked, yet critical part of securing a new role, and provides insights into how professionals can recognize and manage emotions, so they aren't a barrier to landing the position. If you're preparing for a job search, this book will help you to consider the broader landscape, specifically the role your emotions might play in your success."

> – Dr. Dawn Graham, Author of *Switchers: How Smart Professionals Change Careers and Seize Success* and Host of "Dr. Dawn on Careers" on SiriusXM Radio.

"As a psychologist, I have seen how anxiety can destroy a job search and negatively impact the confidence of a job seeker. Herring skillfully walks you though and highlights how to identify and control your emotions during the job search process. I've never seen a job search book that successfully addresses the emotional aspect so effectively."

> – Dr. Alicia H. Clark, PsyD, and Author of *Hack Your Anxiety*

"Every career coach knows the importance of emotions in the job search; however you'd be hard pressed to find a resource that so perfectly articulates and outlines successful strategies for managing your emotions during the search process."

> – Marie Zimenoff, CEO, Resume Writing Academy & Career Thought Leaders

"There is NO OTHER BOOK like this on the market. I will be recommending this to my job candidates so they can take control of their emotions before their interview and land the job!"

> – Sue Burnett, Founder and President of Burnett Specialists, largest employee owned staffing company in Texas

"This is not your ordinary job search book. *Take Control of Your Job Search!* underscores an issue that plays a critical role in a successful job search that is largely unaddressed in career literature. This book will help you discover how your emotions can be a roadblock to landing a job and how to overcome the challenges. The path toward self-discovery and self-awareness offered by this book is invaluable."

   – Dr. Mark Taylor, Dean of the Olin School of Business at Washington University in St. Louis

"I've learned in my 20 years in social services that mastering the emotional component of getting and keeping a job is absolutely critical for people who ultimately gain economic independence. Lauren Herring shares a roadmap for dealing with common emotional setbacks that keep people from taking the next step in their career journey. People at every level and every career path can benefit from the wisdom of *Take Control of Your Job Search!*"

   – Kathy Lambert, Founder and CEO of Connections to Success

As a psychologist and founder of IMPACT Group, I am delighted that Lauren has been able to dissect the nuances of emotions that impact job seekers ability to land a job! Lauren has analyzed and outlined the unique strategies IMPACT Group coaches have used with job seekers over the past 30 years that enable them to remove their emotional barriers to success. This book will change job seekers lives!

   – Laura Herring, Founder of IMPACT Group, and Author of *No Fear Allowed: A Story of Guts, Perseverance and Making an IMPACT.*

TAKE CONTROL
OF YOUR
JOB SEARCH!

10 EMOTIONS
YOU MUST MASTER TO LAND THE JOB

Lauren Herring
CEO of IMPACT Group

Published by Simply Good Press, Montclair, New Jersey

http://www.simplygoodpress.com
Printed in the United States of America

For permissions requests, speaking inquiries, and bulk-order purchase options, visit www.laurenherring.net

Library of Congress Control Number: 2020911234

ISBN-13: 978-1-7352585-1-5 (Paperback)
ISBN-13: 978-1-7352585-0-8 (eBook)

Cover Design: Kate Disabato

Contents

Author's Note

This book was written before everything in our world changed due to the COVID-19 pandemic. It was published during the pandemic, and my hope is that it will be read for many years to come. We are experiencing record levels of unemployment during this crisis. Meanwhile, the emotional toll of joblessness has probably never been higher as our career and financial concerns are now combined with life and death health concerns.

As I write this Author's Note, my heart is breaking for the millions of people that find themselves without a job. I can only imagine what you're feeling as you read this book in the unprecedented labor market. This book is designed to help you become aware of your emotions through each step of your job search and to provide you the framework of support you need as you search for ways to take control of your search and stay focused. Giving in to overwhelming feelings will not get you the job, and your feelings will be stronger and more frequent as the pandemic continues, so be vigilant. Focus, dive deep into your heart and mind, and decide to survive and thrive by committing to follow through with the exercises in this book.

The emotions that this book covers are universal. They are not only part of the job search experience – they are core to the human experience. You are not alone. The guidance and tactics suggested in these pages are based on the collective wisdom of IMPACT Group career coaches with thousands of years of combined accumulated knowledge. And because the emotions are the same even when the circumstances are different, the coaching in this book can be applied in any economic environment.

Even in writing this book, I found I was able to see how some of the exercises and techniques could help me through challenges that I experienced both personally and professionally.

My hope is that no matter the circumstances in which you find yourself when you pick up this book, you will find something that can be applied to your situation that will help you learn and grow.

Move forward. Persevere. And remember, you are never alone!

Introduction

Emotional Elephants

Welcome to *Take Control of Your Job Search! 10 Emotions You Must Master to Land the Job.* I am so excited you have started reading this - it is the first step to Taking Control of your search!

To begin with, I want you to imagine this scene:

Walking into the interview for your dream job, you want to go in feeling calm, confident and ready to share your best self. That's great in theory, but it can be a tall order if the night before you were rejected for another position that you *also* thought was your future dream job! Add to that a prolonged job search with personal and family financial obligations on your mind, and the ups and downs of the process can make you feel like you've lost all control.

I understand - looking for a job can make you feel helpless. If you are in the job market because you were let go from your former employer, or because of a layoff, you probably had very little control over the fact that you are unemployed in the first place. Perhaps it was your choice to be looking, or perhaps this is your first time looking for a job. There are so many things that you can't control about the job search process. You can't make a recruiter call you back. You might be sending in countless applications online with no acknowledgement. And you certainly can't make your dream job magically appear.

There are still many aspects of the job search you can control, however. You can control how you spend your time and you can control how you respond to the challenges and opportunities that come your way. This requires a lot of self-awareness and a willingness to explore your emotions honestly. In short, it requires Emotional Intelligence.

Everyone has an IQ - Intelligence Quotient - and most of us know what that means and even where we are on the scale. Fewer of us are aware of the importance of EQ, or Emotional Intelligence. (Yes, the initials are different but the meaning is parallel). Even fewer still are clear about how our own Emotional Intelligence impacts our relationships with others or how we are perceived in the workplace and in life. If you are looking for a job or a career change, listen up: you need to get clear about your own EQ! It's time to start learning how to grow your awareness of your EQ relating to your emotional state in your job search, which I call Career EQ. How do you do that? Listen to me. I'm Lauren Herring, and I have the privilege of serving as CEO at IMPACT Group, a global career coaching company, serving over 200 Fortune 500 companies. Over the last 30 years, we have helped hundreds of thousands of people find jobs all over the world.

I've seen the good, the bad, and the ugly in job search. Trust me, there are plenty of ugly types of desperate job search strategies. I've watched people wrestle with the challenges of this process - especially the emotional challenges - as they plow through the ups and downs of job search. One of the key learnings I've experienced over the years is that in addition to mastering the traditional job search tactics, the most successful job seekers have also mastered their emotions.

Someone I've seen struggle with this was Joe, a type "triple A plus" personality who was an executive at the top of his career but was laid off because of an acquisition. Previously he was a senior vice president at a large food company, and he *thought* he was in control of his job search because he was in constant action.

He wasn't just sending out hundreds of resumes, he was rewriting his resume for each job application. He wasn't just preparing for job interviews, he was preparing customized spreadsheets and sample job plans to impress potential employers. In between, he was reaching out to his contacts (all of them) and networking like crazy - if there was a person willing to be met, our guy wanted to meet them! On paper and by many job search book standards, this man was doing everything right. He was attacking the job search with the same fervor, attention to detail, and diligence that he had used to build his career. Employers *should* have been lining up with job offers, right? But they weren't, which is why the client came to us for help with his job search.

What was the problem? Why weren't his efforts successful? **His FEAR of not finding a job was driving his job search.** (And making him look like a maniac!)

There was one critical element of the job search Joe was neglecting, and he is not alone. It is one that many people aren't even aware of. This incredibly successful individual was blind to the role that his *emotions* play in the job search. He thought he was doing an excellent job looking for a job, but because he didn't know what he didn't know, he was unaware of how much emotion, in his case, *fear*, was actually in the driver's seat of his search. Unbeknownst to him, anyone who came in contact with him (including potential employers) could sense the fear he was feeling about his job search prospects.

The presence of fear was evident to me too when I first met Joe. I could see immediately that he was spinning his wheels, taking random shots, and every action he took was fueled by fear of the unknown. This is not to say that fear was the sole reason he wasn't landing a new job. But from a self-awareness standpoint, it was the elephant in the room that he wasn't seeing (and it was trampling him). And in this case, what you cannot see, can absolutely hurt you!

Once he began working with us, we convinced him to hit "pause" on his flurry of actions, focus on mindfulness and self-assessment, and use that self-awareness to develop a better job search strategy. Only then did his job search results begin to improve.

So I ask you: are you aware of how you're seen? Do you have a true picture of how you appear to others? Is there a chance, even a small one, that emotions you might not even be aware of, are clouding your judgement? If an executive at the top of his career could be blind to how others were seeing him, might there be a chance that you're missing something too? Or are you currently feeling emotions throughout your job search that are negatively impacting your results? I pose these questions now, at this book's beginning, because self-awareness is a key piece of the job search process.

Zooming out even more - how might gaining this self-awareness of your emotions benefit your life beyond the job search, beyond the job itself, to other areas of your life? If you're willing to develop yourself like this and come to understand your emotions and how they impact the impression you're giving off to others, how might that influence your daily work, your entire career, your marriage, your parenting skills, and more? Learning to zero in on your emotions can create 360 degrees of benefits in your life. Are you willing to examine yourself and your emotions to potentially tap into these rewards?

If so, that willingness alone gives you an edge over other job search candidates and the workforce as a whole. Many people similar to Joe in the story above, are so focused on going through the "proper" motions of the job search, hitting the required steps, aiming for quantity of action over quality (to the point where it becomes action for the sake of action), that they neglect (or are unaware of) the emotional intelligence required to navigate the job search process.

Your emotions matter through the duration of the career cycle, from job search, to being a key determinant in the advancement of your career, all the way through retirement, and even how you look back on your career accomplishments. This book's focus is to show you the role your emotions play in your job search. The ultimate success of your job search will be determined by your ability to understand, manage, and process your emotions, in addition to implementing the right job search strategies. This book will give you the knowledge and tools you need to self-assess whether you're consciously driving your search for your next job (and to what degree) or whether your emotions are actually in the driver's seat. And if the emotions driving your search are negative ones, you will learn how to convert them into positive, empowering ones that increase your probability of success.

String enough successful job searches (and jobs) together and you'll have what you need to build a career where you can feel proud that you've made a positive impact!

Helping people find the right jobs at the right points in their career is core to what our career coaches do at IMPACT Group. Coaches hold up a mirror so people can get a good look at how they come across to others. In addition, a coach acts as cheerleader, motivator, consultant, and guide all in one to help navigate the potentially tricky terrain of the job search. Since looking for a job is usually an unfamiliar experience, having an expert to help with the "tricks of the trade" as well as someone to support you through the often challenging process, can be invaluable. While you might not have a personal coach as you go through your search, the coaching in this book can guide your actions to get the job you want.

When it comes down to it, you don't want just any job, you want the right job! Matching people with the right jobs is also closely linked with my personal mission, to make a positive impact on the world. I believe we can build a better world by empowering people to find and grow great careers that allow them to develop their skills, self-confidence and make a positive difference.

You may be wondering about the lofty sounding connection there - a good job leads to a better world . . . When you think about it though, your job is one of the most important and certainly most time consuming aspects of your life. When you find a great job, grow in your career, or both, it spreads like a positive ripple effect to all other areas of your life. This is similar to the ripple effect that comes from gaining an understanding of your emotions - sensing a pattern yet? You become a better spouse, parent, friend, citizen - everything. How many marriages can be improved, or saved, when one spouse goes from being miserable at their job, to being happy there? Globally, research by Gallup shows that having what you perceive as a "good job," is the number one factor driving overall happiness. This happiness that comes from a job where you're engaged and making a positive impact begins with your job search. outcomes.

If this is the case, then why isn't the topic of emotions in the job search more prevalently covered? Is it because emotions are tied closely to mental health which remains a bit of a taboo topic, especially in corporate circles? Possibly. Or perhaps, as career-driven people we naturally expect that if we work hard enough on the concrete "to-do's" of the job search, our emotions will remain dutifully in the background without getting in our way. Unfortunately, emotions don't work that way.

This book is different from other job search books. Significantly different. Most have historically focused on more concrete job search tactics like resume writing, interviewing, and internet job search strategies and don't cover the subject of emotions. The traditional job search conversation is primarily a skills-based one that is important, but it neglects a vital truth: Employees and job seekers are human beings first, with human emotions. When a human being loses their job, especially when it's the focal point of their life, they might get angry. They might grieve the loss of employment as a core part of their identity. When someone has been searching for months without an offer, they might become overwhelmed, anxious, and paralyzed with fear - maybe so much so that it's hard to even move forward. These waves of emotions might combine into a perfect storm of "stuckness" that a job seeker carries with them into their search, and the fear they're feeling is slapped across their foreheads like a giant scarlet letter. That's not the most appealing first impression in a job interview!

To pull out of this sort of emotional downward spiral, you need more than solely the tools and tactics of the job search (resume, interviewing skills, networking and such), which I call Career IQ. While important, Career IQ alone won't land you the job. You need awareness of your personal emotional state. You need intelligence specifically about the emotional aspects of your job search - you need Career EQ. When we work with people one on one at IMPACT Group, our coaches provide this support. This often comes in the form of guidance on how to proactively and positively address what people are feeling at any point in time, or feedback on how they are coming across emotionally, be it depressed, cynical, angry, obnoxious or a "nervous Nellie". This book is intended to replicate that coaching role (as much as a book realistically can), with knowledge, resources, and activities that will be a vital companion to your job search.

In the first section of the book we'll delve into how to set yourself up for success. In the second, and by far the most significant section, you'll learn about 10 key emotions that can show up in the job search. We start with emotions relating to loss, then move to paralyzing emotions and finally onto gaining momentum. You'll learn how to spot them as they come up and address them head-on including how to deal with the self-talk and beliefs that come with them. Then, you'll get specific tactics you can use to process your emotions and use them to your advantage in your search. The insights and case studies are the collective wisdom that my coaches at IMPACT Group and I have acquired over our 30 years of helping people find jobs. I hope you will see how others' EQ awareness helped them find just the right job along their career journey.

The emotions chapters are specifically designed so you can either read them all the way through or you can flip right to the emotion you are currently experiencing and get the insights and tactics to help you through. In part three of the book you will learn how to apply what you've learned on the job as you move forward in your career. The subject of emotions may seem like an abstract one but make no mistake, this book is ultimately designed for productive, informed, specific action!

The journey of this book won't necessarily be easy. Reaching the level of self-discovery and self-awareness that we are aiming for here is a challenging process. But again, we help thousands of people just like you - job seekers on a mission to find a fulfilling job to ultimately improve their careers - every year. Trust me. We've got them, we've got you, and the destination is worth it.

One important note - emotions are messy, complex, and unpredictable things. Popular concepts like "stages of grief" do not accurately reflect how that process or any other emotion actually works. As a job seeker, you will likely move through multiple emotions like a cat that gets into a stash of catnip - forward, backwards, sideways, and changing directions without warning. That's okay. That's normal. That's human. YOU'RE human!

Finally, I would like to make the distinction about what this book is *not*. This is not intended to be a psychology book, or a replacement for professional therapy or counseling for more serious emotional problems, nor is it meant in any way to be a deep clinical exploration into emotions. My goal is strictly to give you the awareness and guidance you need to help manage your emotions through the potentially stressful process of the job search. From a career standpoint, I will show you how to identify the negative emotions, and the behaviors that reflect those emotions that can get in the way of a successful job search. We'll then focus on, and how to convert those emotions into productive actions that can help you land the job you want today for the career you're working toward tomorrow.

Like I said earlier, this is meant to raise your awareness of a critical piece of missing information for job seekers - whether you're a first timer or a mature worker. This book is my attempt at helping as many people as possible to match their skills and gifts with their career goals, creating a ripple effect of positivity and engagement throughout the workforce and the world!

Part I:

SET YOURSELF UP FOR SUCCESS

"To know thyself is the beginning of wisdom."
-Socrates

Chapter 1

Success In The Job Search

Success in the job search depends on investing time in the right *activities* and *actions* and having the right *attitude*. Tough job markets can skew job seeker perceptions and psychology, making all three of those things a challenge.

In times of high unemployment, it's easy to feel like the odds of success are very low due to the economic climate and the amount of competition for the same job. In a good economy, the stress of the job search may lead many job seekers to the perception that everyone else is "winning" but them.

These thoughts, whether they are fact or fiction, are based on the job seekers' inner beliefs that the odds are stacked against them, that finding a job *should* be easier and faster, that if companies aren't lining up with offers there's "something wrong" with them, and when they receive no replies to their online applications, it must mean that their skills and abilities aren't as stellar as they believed.

Regardless, no matter how great you are, there is more to a successful job search than simply putting your resume out there, sending off online job applications, and waiting for your dream job to fall into your lap. The reality is, a successful job search is a job unto itself. You might be the most talented, skilled, experienced, accomplished person in your industry (according to your mother), but you are not a professional in job searching. Let's look at the external, as well as the internal aspects of the search that you can control which play into your success.

A job search has many moving parts, all susceptible to change based on market and industry conditions, fluctuating technologies, and the emotional reactions of the job seeker throughout the process. A job search can be a massive project to manage. In addition to the tactical to-do's like updating your resume, submitting applications, and preparing for interviews, it includes knowing how to deal with the ups and downs that will be part of your search.

Throughout this chapter, we'll look at ways you can ensure you are getting the right support from external resources, maintain an overall sense of wellbeing, and include the right combination of activities that set you up for success when it comes to staying emotionally healthy throughout the job search.

Building Your Super Team

The most valuable support you'll have during your job search comes from the people around you. I call this your "Super Team." You need to build one. These are the people that you can trust, ones who won't sugar coat the truth and just tell you what you want to hear. Your Super Team should have people who have an understanding of how others see you, people willing to listen to your elevator pitch, and people objective enough to do mock interviews with you. They then need to tell you the truth about how you did in a kind, constructive, and honest way.

When looking for these individuals, take into consideration past relationship history. For instance, if getting negative feedback from your mom drives you up the wall, whether on your career decisions, your choice in romantic partners, or your taste in shoes, then it's best not to ask her for feedback on your job search. Seek out people outside your "emotional walls," which could include former coworkers, a sibling, your pastor, your financial planner, or a neighbor. A spouse will be a crucial player, but because of the interdependence and the stress involved it's not a place to engender objectivity. More on that later. Some people will want their spouse or partner on their Super Team, some won't. **Take a moment to stop and assemble a few names for your Super Team. The sooner you make a list, the sooner you can access their wisdom and compassion.**

I'll refer to this group regularly throughout the book, because you'll want to lean on them as a key part of your success. There's also a resource especially for members of your Super Team (especially for spouses/partners or close family members) in the Appendix, so they can be best prepared on how they can be of service to you.

Maintaining Personal Wellbeing

While there are bound to be challenges in most job searches, part of maintaining strong emotional fitness through the process is to proactively manage your thoughts and your energy. The PERMA model, developed by psychologist Martin Seligman, identifies five "essential elements" that we need to create an ongoing sense of well-being. It stands for: **P**ositive Emotion, **E**ngagement, Positive **R**elationships, **M**eaning, and **A**ccomplishment. This is a simple model that can easily be applied to wellbeing in the job search. Let's break it down.

Positive Emotion: Identify at least one positive emotion every day that you can choose to actively engage in. Gratitude is a good example. No matter what is happening in your job search, no matter how bleak things seem, make a list of things you're grateful for; nothing is too small.

Engagement: You've heard athletes talk about being "in the zone" - that special flow where you're enthusiastic about what you're doing, you lose track of time and you're operating at your peak potential. This might not necessarily apply to sending resumes or filling out job applications, but what other activity can you incorporate into your day to put yourself in this state, for even a brief period of time? A hobby like painting, reading, meditating, exercise, or journaling perhaps? As long as it puts you in the flow, add it to your schedule. Being between jobs doesn't mean that your *only* job is to look for your next one. Taking time for yourself (you - the human being, not the full time job searcher!) creates normalcy and helps keep your emotions in balance.

Positive Relationships: Humans are social creatures and it's important to acknowledge this aspect of yourself, no matter how busy or stressed you are with your job search duties. Make it a priority to find some other humans to be around - preferably ones that you like and who add meaning to your life in some way. Seligman's research showed that those with "meaningful, positive relationships" are happier.

Meaning: Consider how you can invest even a small portion of your time to being of service to others less fortunate than you (p.s. there is *always* someone less fortunate than you) or to a cause bigger than yourself. Adding meaning to your life directly contributes to your sense of well-being. This is a great way to build your job search network as well!

Accomplishment: Celebrate all your daily job search wins, no matter how small. On some days, that might mean literally dragging yourself out of bed and to your computer to bravely check for messages from potential employers. Everything counts, so give yourself credit. Research shows that the forward motion of working toward a goal and celebrating your accomplishments on the way creates momentum, helping you reach that goal faster (and with a happier attitude).

16

Overall, The PERMA Model demonstrates the significant role of emotions, in this case happiness, in our lives. It also reinforces the impact of our daily actions on our emotions.

The Reality Of The Job Search

"I *know* I'm great so why isn't anyone hiring me?"

It's okay to think this. A little healthy self-esteem never hurt anyone! If you're not getting bombarded with job offers, this does not take away from your value. However, it may be a sign that you need to work harder and more strategically to better market your value to potential employers. That's part of your job as a job seeker. Here's the rest of the job description. Take note that it is far more extensive than perusing job ads and submitting job applications!

Job Description Of A Job Seeker

Keep Learning: It is your job to constantly be learning about what is going on in your industry and field of work. Rather than reactively responding to job postings, you should also be researching potential employers. What companies align with your interests, career goals, and values? Who are the key decision makers for jobs you are applying for? What are they looking for in their employees? The more you know about the market, your potential employers, and their needs, the better positioned you'll be to find out where you fit in.

Stay Connected: It's your job to stay connected with your network and your industry, whether via social media, in-person networking, or otherwise, to learn about industry trends, directions, and potential opportunities. This also means keeping your network informed of your job search status so they can support you. Make sure your contacts know what you're looking for and what you have to offer, so that when they do come across something that's a potential match, they will think of you. There's a fine line, of course, between keeping your network informed and pestering them. Aim for follow-up every few weeks, not inbox clogging daily requests.

Maintain a Positive Mindset: It's your responsibility to look inward and examine your beliefs about yourself, your worth, and your potential to get the job you want. It's also your job to adjust those beliefs as needed, especially if they've grown negative and are getting in the way of your job search. While we all do this from time to time, women are especially prone to negative self-talk - (me included!) the loop of negativity, fear, and self-doubt constantly playing in our minds, convincing us that we don't deserve success or happiness. It's important, especially in the job search, to be hyper-aware of such negative beliefs, get them out of the shadows of your mind, because your beliefs drive your thoughts, which in turn drive your actions. So get negative beliefs and thoughts into the light of day and find ways to convert them into positive thoughts. We will get into specifics on how to do this later.

Are any negative beliefs coming up as you're reading this? If so, stop right now, get a journal or notebook, and write them down. For each negative thought that you've written, write next to it FIVE positive beliefs about yourself (they do not have to be connected). The best way to banish shadows is by shining a light at them!

Practice Gratitude: Also in your job description as a job seeker is to develop a consistent practice of giving thanks for what you do have and celebrating even the smallest wins during your job search process. It has proven time and time again, that an "attitude of gratitude" and recognition of your successes can build confidence and impact the quality and ultimately the outcome of your actions.

Don't Take Things Personally: Yes, this might sound trite, and it's definitely easier said than done, but let me tell you loud and clear: your resume, job application, and interview skills do NOT reflect your worth as a human being. Learn how to compartmentalize "you: job seeker" from "you: whole person." Depersonalize the overall job search process. Rejection, no matter how bitter a pill it can be to swallow, is not a personal judgment against you. It's simply the impression by the hiring manager that someone else was a better fit for the job. Don't read into it beyond that.

Look at each "failure" as an opportunity to identify what you *did* have control over on your end, take an honest look at how you did in those areas, and make adjustments. For example, you do *not* have control over whether another candidate is a better match for the skills and experience of the position. But you *do* have control over how much time you put into your interview preparation. As my mother, Laura Herring (the founder of IMPACT Group) said in her book *"No Fear Allowed"* - the "F" in failure is for "feedback."

Stay Healthy: The physical body of the person seeking the job has needs too. When you ignore those needs, you're putting yourself at a huge disadvantage, like trying to win the *Indy 500* in a broken down car. With all the information and resources available to help you maintain a basic good state of health, I won't go into great detail other than to remind you that good health generally includes a balance of proper nutrition, daily physical activity, and some type of mind-body health (such as yoga, meditation, or spirituality in some form). Prioritize your health like all the other pieces of your job search.

Get Your Finances in Order: Being out of work can be a financially stressful time, depending on how much of a financial cushion you may or may not have. We'll discuss this more in the chapter on anxiety, but if you are worried about money, that anxiety *will* come through to potential employers, especially in interviews. One of your responsibilities as a job seeker, is to do everything in your power to calm those worries. I recommend connecting with a financial planner early on if possible to get help understanding your financial situation. Also, it's important to be realistic about the length of time a job search could take. It's not unusual to underestimate the amount of time it will take to find a new job, which could have a lasting effect on your long term finances if you don't make adjustments to your lifestyle early on.

Another consideration may be taking on a "side hustle" of some sort - a method of earning money to make ends meet so you can stay clear headed and focused in your job search, and avoid making bad choices out of financial desperation. Having a side hustle will also prevent you from sitting and staring at your computer screen hour after hour, day after day, in a state of acute anxiety, holding your breath as you wait to hear from a recruiter. A life in purgatory is no life at all, so don't allow any side hustle to keep you from landing the *right* job down the line. Think of a side hustle as an anxiety-lessening tool if this is a serious concern for you. I recommend doing this from day one - NOT months down the line when the bills are piling up and you have no choice but to accept the first job offer that comes along. Why not give yourself that financial flexibility from day one so you can then move forward without that worry, like an elephant you're carrying around on your back?

Be Honest with Yourself: The entire search can be a learning process. Here are some factors to self-assess as you move forward through the job search process. I recommend journaling or reflecting on these questions regularly through your search.

1. What do you need to continue doing that's bringing you results?

2. What could you be doing more of?
3. What do you need to start doing?
4. What do you need to stop doing?
5. Who else can you invite in to help you with these tasks?

Throughout this book I will present several topics for job search related discovery, any of which can benefit from journaling and reflection. I hope you will put in the time and thoughtful effort a successful job search warrants.

That's the baseline description of your responsibilities as a job seeker - the behaviors you can consistently commit to that will put you in the best possible position to market yourself to potential employers.

The reality is, being without a job is a mental and physical stressor that can trigger the full range of emotions covered in this book and then some. Through no fault of your own, you may end up on an emotional roller coaster leaving you feeling out of control. Trying to convince yourself that what you're feeling is "no big deal," and denying the problem only allows the emotions to build up with no outlet. One rejection might not be the end of the world, but 20 per week can do a number on your psyche. The constant grind and build-up of negative emotions, sometimes with no end in sight, can leave you feeling defeated and hopeless. Left to fester long enough, these emotions can stop you in your tracks, paralyze your forward progress, and when certain emotions cross the line into more serious states like chronic anxiety and stress, they can cause physical harm.

My coaches and I have seen this happen to quite a few very successful people, and it can be debilitating. It's terrible for the job seeker, their family, everyone around them, and even for the potential employers they're in contact with. Nobody deserves that. This book exists because I don't want you to have to go through it, or if you do, I don't want you to do it alone. Remember, this book is a virtual coaching tool of sorts, to help you spot and stop the cycle of negative, paralyzing emotions before it potentially damages your career future. Depending on your own personal journey, you may want to consider using other behavioral health tools such as counselors, therapists and peer support groups.

Emotions are undeniable. But with the right self-awareness, knowledge, and job search tools and tactics, they are also controllable. I'm glad you're here reading this and on behalf of my coaches and myself, thank you for trusting us to help you!

Chapter 2

Brand Yourself

Self-awareness is core to every phase of the job search. The better you understand who you are, strengths and weaknesses, and the career goals you're out to accomplish in the short and long term, the smoother your job search will go. Knowing yourself is also at the heart of "personal brand," which for the purposes of this book, means the impression you make on potential employers.

Personal brand is core to Career EQ. Think about it this way: when you know who you are, and you wear your personal brand with pride and confidence, it can serve as protective armor through the ups and downs of the job search, especially as various emotions pop up along the way. For that reason, personal brand, and how it connects with the emotions and tactics of the job search, will be an ongoing theme in this book. I believe that personal brand is such a powerful tool in ensuring strong and consistent Career EQ that it is the one tactic in the job search process that I will explore thoroughly in this chapter.

Know thyself; brand thyself, and give yourself the competitive edge in your job search!

Branding Yourself

In business, every time a product or service is sold, there is a branding process attached to that sale. The goal of the process is to let the customer know what the product is, why it stands out from the rest, what it can do, and why they need it. In the job search, *you* are the product.

What Do You Want To Do?

In order to be clear about your personal brand, the first step is making sure you are clear about what you want. If you're not clear about your goals, then it's probably difficult to "sell yourself" in a compelling way to potential employers as a solution to their problems.

A team member who has been with our company for about seven years, recently let us know that she's ready for a change. Feeling uninspired by her work, she knew she didn't want to be writing resumes in the long term, but hadn't the slightest clue as to what she *did* want to do.

This is a common issue in people doing something they have mastered. They're bored with their job but haven't yet done the inner work to figure out the next level of their career and what they need to do to get there. They're not actively preparing to move up the career ladder.

This preparation involves self-assessment, research, and learning. To make the leap to your next career level, you must immerse yourself in the vision of what that level is and, step by step, everything you need to *do* and *know* to get there.

When we coach job seekers like the individual I mentioned above, we'll often use a career assessment like the Myers-Briggs Type Indicator or O*NET Interest Profiler - both available for free online should you desire to use them. These are a starting point to assess the person's skills to see how they match up with their goals or help identify what the long term career goals are. Then it's important to determine what is needed for alignment. This could mean taking classes, expanding their horizons by reading free material on the internet, acquiring new certifications or other continuing education, or, in some cases, volunteering for projects within the company that align with their new goals.

If you want to reach certain career goals it's your responsibility to develop those skills. whether employed or not. For example, after reviewing her assessment results, our team member has taken on the role of communications lead on a substantive software conversion happening within our company. Rather than sitting and waiting for her next career opportunity to drop into her lap, she is now being proactive, converting her career potential into actual skills and experience that will make her more marketable.

How can you follow in her footsteps, and identify what you want to do next in your career, research your job options, and learn any new skills that you'll need to perform it? There are many great resources out there that focus solely on career change and career assessment, so I'm not going to go into depth here; however, here are a few thoughts to get you started if this is something that is relevant to you.

Self-Assessment

1. What do you want to do next in your career?
2. Why?
3. What do the assessments say could be a good career fit and do any of those options excite you?
4. What do you enjoy doing professionally and personally?
5. What are your greatest strengths and achievements?
6. How do they support your career goals?
7. What weaknesses do you have that might hold you back from these goals?
8. What is your plan for managing those weaknesses?

Research and Learning

1. What industries and job options are available based on your goals and strengths?
2. What new job skills might be required for these job options?

3. How will you obtain these skills (online learning, in-person course, books, etc.)?

What Are You Doing To Brand Yourself To Employers?

What are you doing to present yourself in the best possible light? What are you doing to get your "whole self" into focus? Investing in a healthy dose of self-awareness is as important of a job search tool as more concrete tactics like resume writing and interview preparation.

Are you presenting yourself in a way that focuses on what you can do for employers rather than the reverse? The personal branding process, in many ways, is not about telling potential employers why you're great. It's about telling them what you're going to do to make their company great. When you're invited to a party you don't ask what they're going to be serving, you ask what you can bring. Same principle.

The clearer you are about your brand, the better the results will be throughout the job search. Even as your story changes based on the progression of your career, who you are at the center of that story, your core value, will remain consistent. Your brand is the promise of what you will bring to a company and how you will add value.

Here are some questions to guide your thinking as you begin your branding process.

Brand Impression Questions:

1. What is the one thing you want to be known for?
2. What are you currently doing to build a compelling brand impression for employers around that "one thing"?

3. How can you improve on that impression? For instance, the use of video is key in branding. Are you using enough of it? In today's job search, digital brand IS your first impression.?

4. What personal obstacles need to be overcome and/or additional skills gained to create a more compelling brand impression?

5. What tools, knowledge and/or resources can you actively seek out to get past those obstacles?

The concept of personal brand is such an important one that throughout this book you'll see it addressed in micro sections called "Brand Angle." The goal is to help you better connect the dots between how successfully dealing with your emotions while searching for a job directly impacts the personal brand impression you're making on others, most importantly, potential employers.

What Brand Impression Do You Need To Make?

This brings us to building a brand impression that will help support your job search goals! To assess your current brand impression, it's important to know what has worked for you in your career up until now.

1. What parts of your current/last job (the one you're moving away from) did you like the most?

2. What parts of your current/last job did you like the least?

3. Of all the positions you've had in your career, which one was your favorite? Why?

4. If someone talked to your last manager, what would they say is the best thing about you?

5. If that person talked with your coworkers at your last job, (or your family and friends) what would they say they appreciated the most about you?
6. Which three things (personality traits, skills, talents, etc.) are your unique value?
7. What are 2-3 accomplishments you are most proud of both personally and professionally?
8. What's the "weirdest" thing about you that others find positive?
9. What are the things you're looking for in your next job?
10. Pick your favorite magazine in your industry and imagine an article written about you in five years. Summarize what the article says.
11. What needs to happen career wise for you between now and then to make that article a reality?

The goal of these questions is to help you recognize who you are at your best, especially during the job search. Right now, especially if you've been recently laid off, you might be feeling far from your career best. But the double-edged sword is that to land your next job, you need to present your best impression. This is where the branding process becomes one of your most valuable search tactics.

Getting Feedback

Abbi needed a change of scenery in her career, but was plagued with self-doubt about stepping outside the world she knew and venturing into the unknown. The negative self-talk was taking over her brain: *What am I thinking? Am I really qualified to do anything else? Who would ever hire me?*

As a way of combating her fear of the unknown and ensuring a smooth career transition, Abbi wrote a list of all her strengths and positive character traits - every single thing she could think of. She also asked her Super Team, comprised of friends, peers, and past clients to draw up the same lists about her.

Abbi was overwhelmed by the results of her request! The feedback and words of praise she received from her peers, employees and everyone else she'd asked, allowed her to see her gifts, skills, and potential in a whole new light. She not only became confident about her search, but also genuinely excited all over again about this new chapter in her life, especially when seeing it through the eyes of her greatest supporters.

These steps that Abbi took - making a list of all her strengths and positive traits, and then requesting that others who know her do the same, are integral in the process of branding yourself.

Go Deeper

Go the extra mile and deepen the branding process by looking for potential alignment between things like your purpose, core values, and goals. As you meet with companies throughout your search, you'll be able to match up how your purpose connects with a company's mission and vision.

For instance, if you're passionate about preserving the environment and a potential employer's mission is to reduce pollution, that sort of value alignment, one that touches heart and gut, can be a powerful connector. The better you know yourself, your mission, your why, and where you stand ideologically, the more potential doors of connection and rapport that you can open between yourself and potential employers.

At IMPACT Group, for instance, my radar is constantly tuned to candidates who are out to make a positive difference in the world. When a candidate connects with me authentically on that level, self-marketing is far from impersonal or "sale-sy." It is an alignment of core values. It's you and the potential employer coming together to see how working together, you can both feel confident that it's a great match.

How's Your Search Swagger?

The most thoroughly developed brand impression will fall flat without self-confidence. How well are you wearing your brand impression? Are you showing up in your search with enough confidence as if to you entered the room looking like a million bucks or like you just closed the deal of a lifetime?

If not, what's missing in your branding process? Did you go back as far as possible in your career and identify all the things you were doing when you were at your career best? Are you clear on your short and long-term career goals and what is needed to reach them? If you're short on swagger, the reason is most likely lack of clarity or a missing piece of information that could be the key to unlocking your dream job. How's your job search swagger these days on a scale of one to ten?

Brand Angle: Supersize Your Swagger

1. **Who are you at your best? Take some time to journal or make notes about your very best qualities, both personally and professionally - the traits and skills that make you feel the best about yourself.**

2. **What awesomeness do you bring to your job that others perhaps do not?**

3. **How have you been successful at work in the past? List all the ways!**

Biggest Takeaway

As we move into the emotions chapters, the most important thing to bring with you is this: self-awareness. Start thinking about who you are (personally and in your career), your core values, personal mission in life, your strengths as an employee, and the value you bring to an organization that can help them grow and meet their goals. Remember to recruit a Super Team that can help you build your personal brand and support you as you're negotiating the job search process.

Even with all the swagger in the world, it's very easy to feel alone during a job search. It might seem like you're the only person on earth suffering the constant, daily monotony of pointing and clicking your way through the job search, sending email after email into what sometimes seems like a black hole, the anxiety of waiting in purgatory for a response - any response - and the grief and anger of rejection. It might seem like everyone else is employed except you. And the worst part is, you might be doing all the right things, but getting no acknowledgment for doing so.

These feelings are normal. Looking for a job is a stressful time. You're about to pick up valuable tactics to deal with these challenges. A successful job search requires hard work. But with the right knowledge, tactics, and support system - you will be positioned to succeed!

Part II

Loss Emotions

"Successful people have fear, successful people have doubts, and successful people have worries. They just don't let these feelings stop them."
—T. Harv Eker

The Emotions Chapters

Welcome to the core of Career EQ - the emotions chapters!

You're about to get a firsthand look at how our career coaches expertly guide job seekers through the process of:

1. Spotting emotions that are potentially hindering their job search efforts.
2. Processing those emotions.
3. And when possible, converting them into productive emotions.

Each chapter focuses on an emotion and is structured around an initial assessment, actual stories from IMPACT Group clients so you can see how these 10 emotions show up in real life and how they affect the job search, and along with each story, tactics you can implement when you're experiencing each emotion to successfully move forward. (Names and some details have been changed for anonymity purposes.)

Because the goal of this book is to replicate the live experience of working with a career coach as best as possible, you'll find mini-activities called *Take Control Checkpoints* throughout each chapter to help you apply what you've learned as you go. Knowledge without application is a car without gas. You can have the fanciest most expensive car in the world, but if it doesn't start, it's nothing but an expensive lawn decoration! As you go through the book, be prepared to reflect and dig deep to get the most out of your career journey.

Together, the stories, theory, and application you're about to receive are the best possible representation of what it's like to work one-on-one with an IMPACT Group coach as you navigate the ups and downs of your job search. So, grab a journal, your tablet, laptop, or however you prefer to reflect introspectively, get comfortable, and get excited - because you're about to get access to our very best Career EQ!

Chapter 3

Grief & Sadness

The loss of something that just yesterday felt normal and provided security - your job - can be totally uncharted emotional territory. The loss of a job is closely connected to the loss of your identity (personally and professionally), your financial stability, and in some cases, both of these things if you are the family breadwinner. On some level, you might be afraid of never again regaining those roles or that sense of security in your life. This loss of security can trigger feelings of grief and sadness over what has been lost, even temporarily. It's important that we never underestimate the presence of grief associated with a job loss of any kind or for any reason. Whether the job loss was unexpected or a career move is proactively planned, any transition of that magnitude where familiarity and routine are severely disrupted involves some derivative of grief.

Psychologist George Kohlrieser says that, "Grieving is a necessary part of healthy development. The loss and pain we work through become part of our identities, and this is why being able to deal with separations in our lives is vital for our own growth." While the loss you're experiencing might feel endless at this point, what we know about grief and the grieving process is that it can eventually open doors to great opportunity. Let's go find that opportunity together.

Assess:
Are grief and sadness showing up in your job search?

1. Are the same negative thoughts playing on a continuous loop in your mind, making it difficult to focus on forward momentum?
2. Are you experiencing any life changes - to your daily routine, appetite, sleep, or interactions with others?
3. Are you not showing up fully in other roles in your life (spouse, parent, friend, etc.)?
4. Do you find yourself feeling numb about most things you used to get pleasure or joy from?
5. Are you hearing yourself leading with your grief and sadness when talking about your job search to others?

If you answered yes to any of the above questions - it's okay. You're in the same boat with many other job seekers who are feeling the same way and experiencing some of the same things right now.

How Grief and Sadness Show Up In The Job Search

How do you navigate grief and sadness? First, it's important to understand how grief and sadness show up in the job search, as well as the overall distinction between the two. For our purposes here, grief refers to the acute loss of the job and the myriad of emotions that can be felt in the moment, including but not limited to anger, bitterness, denial, or depression.

Sadness for what has been lost is a residual feeling that can also set in at the time of the loss. But for many job seekers, it is often a cumulative, long-term emotional effect - one that can feel like spiraling down a well. It can set in after weeks or months of job searching with no apparent results. If grief is the electric shock, sadness is the muscle pain that settles in afterward; a pain that, in order to pass, must be acknowledged and given time and space to heal. It begins, however, with the grieving of the separation between you and a great source of security and stability in your life - your job.

Loss Of Identity

An important question to consider: "If you are what you do, who are you when you don't do it anymore?" For many, a "job" is so much more than a place to go every day and collect a paycheck. A job, your position within a company, your work, is wrapped up tightly with how you see yourself in a broader sense and how you believe others see you, especially your loved ones. It's related to professional and even personal fulfillment. Therefore, when a job loss happens, as much as you're told not to take it personally, it feels almost impossible not to do so, and it can feel insulting when someone suggests it's not personal.

For instance, if someone has been an engineer at a certain company for decades, and they identify themselves as such, and now suddenly, especially at a later age, that rug is ripped out from under them, a big piece of how they see themselves is now gone.

When loss of job morphs into a feeling of loss of identity, the self-talk that is triggered can become intensely personal - "you're no good," "you're not worthy" and other variations of imposter syndrome (the inability to believe that your success has been legitimately earned). In this way, loss of identity can show up as a significant offshoot of grief in the job search.

The loss of a job might be an isolated, singular event, but the emotional chain reaction it triggers is not nearly as tidy. The ways in which grief and sadness show up in the job search can touch all areas of your life. They can be surprising and also extremely unpredictable.

Loss Of Your Planned Future

Think back to when you started your last job – that was probably an exciting time. You presumably had been preparing every step along the way, whether that was studying diligently in school, dreaming of the day when you'd finally have the opportunity to show the working world what you're made of, or making all the right moves up the ladder. Regardless, you finally took that crucial step toward the next phase in your career.

So what happens when that future is yanked away, when you are laid off or fired from your job, or maybe you simply realize that your job is not everything you hoped it would be. It might feel not only like the loss of a job but in a way, the loss of your career future. Realistically you know there will be another job but in the moment, it can feel like the end of the world. The level of rejection feels deep.

Even if you never felt like this prior job was your "dream job," just the fact that you were rejected from it feels like a personal affront (even though in all likelihood, on your employer's side it was purely a "business decision"). And if it's the first time this has happened to you, the grief of losing your job for the first time can feel particularly raw and intense.

Depending on the circumstances, additional layoffs can also be devastating, bringing with them that same sudden onslaught of uncertainty. Whether it's your first job or your fifteenth, whether you're in your twenties or your sixties, the grief and feeling of uncertainty in your future that comes with a job loss can make you feel defeated and less than motivated to engage in the job search process.

Loss Of Community

The loss of a job can also mean grieving the loss of connection with colleagues and friends in the workplace or the surrounding work culture.

In tech companies especially, where "work" can be a 24/7 culture - a life unto itself with everything from nap pods to 24/7 food and dry cleaning services - employees can feel like they're losing their home away from home. There's also grieving the loss of potential career path of opportunities with the company, the career storylines you envisioned, and goals you set.

Grief is grief, it's sadness about being rejected, and it can lead to an individual "checking out" of the job search.

Tactics To Overcome Grief & Sadness

Reconnect With Your Inner Rockstar

Lori felt very comfortable in her role as Chief Marketing Officer of a Fortune 100 beverage company - a household name. She'd been employed by the corporate giant for over a decade and in that time had received six promotions up to her current role. From her vantage point, finally in the C-Suite, she'd "arrived" in her career and the possibilities were endless! She was well on her way to implementing the marketing strategy she had set, and her vision was coming into focus.

Then, like a freight train suddenly barreling down a quiet street, a new CEO came along and let Lori go. Just like that. Lori was blindsided with a mix of shock, fear, sadness, and ultimately, a massively shaken confidence and sense of self. In that one moment, she felt like all her prior successes had been wiped out and were just empty words on a resume.

Lori was deep into the grief process. She was grieving the perception of her loss of her identity as a successful executive as well as the vision for the future she'd crafted around that role for herself, her team and the company overall. The shock and sadness she felt and projected made it nearly impossible for her to move forward in her search for a new job until she found a way to process the grief over what could have been and moved forward to what could be.

To do this, Lori needed to dig deep and reconnect with who she was at her "career best." She tapped into the successful person she was at her core – the one who was on the fast track and regularly recognized for her accomplishments – rather than sinking into the identity of the temporarily laid off person she was now. This involved a good amount of visualization, journaling, and even querying her former colleagues about the things they valued the most about her so she could see herself in the same positive light that others did. Taking these steps helped her process her grief and move forward in the job search.

Through the fog and confusion of grief and sadness from a sudden job loss, it can be difficult to see yourself and what you have to offer in a positive light. If a top executive like Lori can feel this way, it's only natural that you may as well. It's not as if you can simply flip a "rockstar" switch and feel like one. You're only human after all. Take the time you need to grieve the loss, then, like Lori did, visualize yourself in better times when you *were* rocking your career, remember what that felt like, how much others appreciate your gifts, and then ask former colleagues what they liked about working with you (use the questions in Chapter 2 as cues). By reconnecting with and doubling down on your personal brand, you will likely find the spark that will ignite your search.

Brand Angle: Reconnect with Your Inner Rockstar

Contact at least one former colleague and ask them what they valued the most about working with you. Reflect on their answer - does it surprise you? How can you use their response as a trigger to help reconnect with your career best self, your inner rockstar?

Experience The Pain

Marco, an environmental scientist, was a single dad and therefore sole breadwinner for himself and his eight-year-old twin daughters. At first when he was laid off, Marco was optimistic and even jovial about the job search ahead, believing that everything would resolve itself quickly and he and his daughters would be just fine. But as the weeks and then months dragged on and still no job offers, he dug himself into the deep emotional hole of sadness, growing silent and withdrawing from those trying to help and support him. Burrowing in his emotions, Marco did not let anyone or anything in or out.

As his job search results only worsened, Marco found himself at a crossroads - either deal with his emotions head on, or risk the life and future he had with his girls. As a loving dad and also wanting to set a positive example for his girls, he opted for the Career EQ route, and chose to confront his emotions. In doing so, he ended up unpacking the grief and resulting sadness triggered by the loss of his job.

That's when it hit Marco – by attempting to initially suppress his grief over his job loss, he had been following in his own father's footsteps! He recalled how his father's natural tendency of pushing down emotions eventually led to heart disease and sadly a fatal heart attack. He knew analytically as a scientist and also intuitively through this new "EQ ah-ha" about his dad, that he needed to take tangible action to feel his pain in order to move forward and avoid the same tragic fate.

Marco developed a structured job search daily action plan that included one or two brief interludes to focus on his grief. Most of his routine revolved around job search tactics that moved him forward in the marketplace, but also key to this routine was space to feel his grief. He set specific time on his calendar for this, which allowed himself to feel it, journal about it, talk about it and even yell about. After a week or two of this routine, he felt much more whole again and was comfortable with the grieving time being on an as needed basis. This strategy ultimately guided him from where he was, right back into the workforce within three months.

Not allowing yourself to feel your grief can be one of the biggest dangers to healthy emotional processing of any loss and therefore a big obstacle to your job search. Recognize and honor the loss you've just gone through - don't deny its reality.

Get Closure

Grant was a leader who for several years, had been on an expat assignment in Asia. Based on his exemplary work in Asia, the company promoted and relocated him to Brazil where he'd be exposed to even higher level career opportunities. For most employees, this would be a positive leveling up and for Grant it was too - at first. However, once in Brazil, Grant found himself experiencing sometimes profound levels of grief and sadness and was baffled as to why, especially with everything going so well in his career. The relocation had been entirely voluntary and a positive step up for him. Intellectually, he knew he "should" be over the moon. After some introspection though, what he finally realized was that he had failed to get closure with the very tribal communities of people he'd bonded with during his time in the eastern countries. He and his family had become ingrained in the cultures of those communities, and so it finally hit him that he had never done a proper goodbye.

To resolve these feelings of grief and loss so he could move forward in his new position, one year later Grant flew back east, had a celebration with his teams in those countries and finally closed the door properly on the experience. Even though the decision to leave his job was one hundred percent his, that did not make Grant automatically immune to feelings of grief and loss. His feelings were so strong that they prevented him from successfully moving forward in his new job.

It's important to acknowledge and value the relationships formed in your old job, rather than rushing forward into your new workplace relationships. Take stock, decide who you wish to stay connected to and at the same time, which relationships have run their course and therefore deserve a proper goodbye.

Take Control Checkpoint: **Loose Ends**

Are there any relationship loose ends from any of your prior jobs that deserve closure? Write down a few. What action step can you take today toward getting that closure?

Find Something You Can Control

As you're actively processing the emotions of the loss, even in cases of intentional or expected job change where these feelings may surprise you, do not use the sadness as an excuse to entirely shut down your tactical job search efforts. The level, intensity, and length of time that grief and other emotions show up, can be directly correlated to the control you're able to exert on your transition.

One of the big challenges of grieving job loss is the feeling that so much is out of your control. So a way to soften the blow may be to find something you CAN control about the process. For instance, cleaning out your desk on the day you are leaving or setting aside time to say goodbye to your coworkers. Later on, this can be dedicating a certain amount of time towards networking, committing to continuous learning within your industry, or exercising a number of times per week. Take action steps in your job search as soon as possible, because taking even small but consistent steps is a way of exerting such control.

Take Control Checkpoint: **Controlled Change**

Make a list of all the things in your life and your job search that you CAN control. (See above for examples) When you're feeling overwhelmed, refer to this list, choose a controllable activity and do it.

Let It Out

A significant aspect of grieving is looking back on and honoring what you once had. Leaning on your Super Team is another valuable tactic to process grief. Finding people that you can speak openly with and not feel judged can help to relieve the burden. Expressing your feelings is paramount in "unpacking" the complete experience - what you had (the job) and your feelings about losing it.

You can also do this through journaling. Journaling is one of the most valuable tools available for processing grief and sadness as well as all the other emotions in this book. Write it down, acknowledge it, say goodbye to it, even write a letter to yourself about what you learned and what you want to do differently in your next job.

No Apologies

Accept the fact that you are grieving a loss just like any other and don't feel obligated to apologize to others as you go through what is a very normal process. Don't try to rush the process, simply to appear "okay" or to appease others who might have a different timeline in mind for grieving a job loss (whether based on their own experience or maybe they've never lost a job so they don't understand).

Baby Steps

While honoring your grieving process and giving yourself the time and space you need, it's also important to take action to avoid getting stuck in this emotion (thus halting your job search). Sadness is only deepened by stagnation, so movement - any movement at all (even when it is *so* hard to get moving) - counteracts that. Small actions to move you forward might be watching webinars, reading books, or listening to podcasts, either about the job search or relating to your industry.

Creating clear action steps as part of an action plan, will help you shift your energy from sadness to forward momentum. It's like the flywheel analogy, described by Jim Collins in his book *Good to Great*. It takes great effort to push a heavy flywheel into motion, but as you keep pushing, even in small bursts, the wheel goes faster and faster. Eventually, the flywheel is able to create its own momentum and spin on its own. Each action you take toward your next job search, even when it's the last thing you want to do and no matter how small, will contribute to that overall momentum. Keep pushing, even a little at a time!

Seek Out New Opportunities

Try reframing the loss of a job as an opportunity to broaden your horizons. Is there a passion you've never pursued that you can turn into a career? Perhaps this is the beginning of your "encore career" - something you've always wanted to do but never had time to before now, something less demanding and for many of you "less corporate" than your job.

This might be coaching sports at the local high school, becoming self-employed, or pursuing a personal passion in a professional way (such as playing an instrument or working in the sports industry). Or you might be drawn toward making a positive impact via work in the nonprofit sector.

The opportunities, once you zoom out from the acute state of separation and loss, are truly endless!

Key Points:

- Grieving is an important part of moving forward and personal growth and is a key element in job changes.

- The loss of the job may be what causes the initial sense of loss, but the deeper sense of loss may be grieving the sense of identity or the community that came with the job. Workplace relationships are much more than "just work" and require their own processing.

- Be aware of unproductive behaviors and keep sadness in check as job loss grief is a risk factor for depression.

- The common denominators of the tactics for processing grief and sadness are not denying it or bottling it up, but rather finding a way to take action, no matter how small, to move through it.

Chapter 4

Anger

Emotions aren't linear, they don't run in cycles, and they're often unpredictable. Anger is a primal emotion, but it is rarely an island unto itself. It's sometimes a secondary emotion to feelings of loss, fear, rejection, resentment, and other kinds of hurt. Anger might be the emotion you're feeling on the surface, but in the job search, it's almost always powered by other emotions beneath the surface that will also need to be processed for your next job search to be a success.

Assess:
Is anger showing up in your job search?

1. **Do you have recurring thoughts about the unfairness of your situation?**
2. **Do you find that you are blaming others, yourself, or the 'system' for the fact you have not yet reached your job search goal?**
3. **Have you lashed out at your loved ones for no reason?**
4. **When you feel angry, are you able to see the big picture?**
5. **Are you spending more time fuming about "what happened" (how you were let go from your last job), compared to the time you're actively spending on your job search?**

How Anger Shows Up In The Job Search

Rage

Anger typically shows up soon after a job loss, usually right after you get the bad news. How your employer handles the situation can make all the difference in the types of emotions triggered, and the strength and duration of those emotions. If you're blindsided and don't see the job loss coming, you'll most likely be understandably shocked, and the anger you feel can run stronger and run longer. A layoff can even show up as outright rage, especially for high performers who *really* didn't see it as a possibility.

Anger that occurs with a job change may be very appropriate and justified, but it being justified or not has no real bearing on whether it helps or hurts a situation – only what we do with the emotion and how we process it actually impacts us.

Feelings of resentment and rage can make it challenging for people to engage positively in their search for a new job, especially if they're bringing with them that cloud of negative energy. This black cloud then colors their vision in the new job search. Therefore, we must get control of even justified anger.

Take Control Checkpoint: **Lashing Out**

Stop for a moment and ask yourself: Have I recently lashed out uncharacteristically at people? Even people I love?

In Silence

When you're searching for a job, sitting in front of a computer in isolation, sending out application after application and resume after resume, and getting no response in return - it can create frustration and after enough time, anger and resentment. These feelings of bitterness at the world can throw up spike strips very quickly, flattening the tires of forward motion in your job search.

If you're not tuned into these angry internal thoughts and feelings, they can hijack the external image you're presenting to others. What kind of first impression are you presenting, whether in an interview or while networking, with a layer of anger simmering just beneath the surface?

Projection

Anger can be projected inward as well as outward. When anger is turned inward it can become self-destructive and turn into self-blame, which is a discharge of anger. This can turn into self-sabotage, where you're secretly beating yourself up for "failing" and losing your job, and therefore unconsciously undermining your efforts toward getting a new job. Anger, turned inward, can lead to depression and can immobilize you.

When anger is projected externally, it can land on others, often those who in reality had nothing to do with the initial job loss. If you're unaware that you're still holding onto resentment surrounding your job loss, it can be all too easy to "take it out" on your spouse, loved ones, and friends, sometimes without even realizing it.

Entitlement

Even though the job loss might not be your fault, it is rarely personal. While you very well might not have deserved it, the fact is, the lack of control that happens when your livelihood and day-to-day routine are suddenly ripped away feels *really* personal because you bear the consequences.

For mature workers who are reaching the end of their earning lifetime, it might feel as if someone is intentionally messing with their retirement plan. For younger workers, it might feel like the employer is derailing their future career plans.

This lack of control leads to anger which can turn into a sense of entitlement. You might think, "I did great for this company! I did nothing wrong and therefore I shouldn't have to lift a finger to find another job. Somebody *owes* me a job!" You may be correct, but that will have no bearing on your job search and getting stuck in thoughts like these will absolutely hamper job search efforts moving forward.

Tunnel Vision

The "Broaden-and-Build Theory of Positive Emotions," developed by Barbara Fredrickson, states that when you are thinking negatively, you start to have tunnel vision and see fewer and fewer positive possibilities around your situation. Whereas when you have positive thoughts, you're open to more possibilities. Therefore, in the context of a job search, if you're so angry at your previous company for laying you off and harboring an "I'll show them!" mentality, you will be less likely to be open to the possibility of getting a great new job at a company you feel positively about.

Tactics To Overcome Anger

Turn Emotions Into Words

When Rick was unexpectedly laid off from his job, he was angry. He decided to deal with his anger by setting a goal of getting re-employed as quickly as possible - to prove to his former employer that he didn't need them and was better off without them. His attitude was clearly, "Those idiots messed up BIG time when they let ME go, I'll show them!"

Powered by all that angry energy, Rick was ready to hit the job search path full speed ahead! The sooner he could exact revenge on his previous employer, the better. The problem is, of course, no potential employer is terribly interested in interviewing - let alone hiring - the incredible hulk. "Revenge" is not a great answer to the interview question, "Why do you want to work for us?" Even if you don't actually say the word "revenge" it still will be present in your overall aura and vibe.

To be successful in finding his next job, Rick would need to redirect all this impatient, angry energy in a more effective, forward thinking way; a way that would help him actually get a job. He had the right tactical intention, to get back out there and get a new job. It was the - "I'll show them!" - emotion *behind* the intention that needed adjusting.

Rick was especially enthusiastic about the networking piece of the job search process. He was itching to pick up the phone, send out emails, reach out to his contacts on social media, and even schedule one-on-one meetings to gather employer leads.

Fortunately for Rick, he took the time to practice mock interviewing, and a roadblock popped up when he found himself hung up with the question "Why did you leave your last job?" which triggered his anger all over again. At this point,

Rick had the self-awareness to admit that he actually was not ready to start the public side of his job search after all. He saw that until he invested the time and energy in processing his anger, that the emotion would be a liability in the process.

He chose to accomplish this via journaling and talking to support people in his life, including his best friend and his wife. Through these tactics, along with some others, Rick was able to put a voice to his feelings and get all those angry thoughts out that he'd been playing in a continuous loop in his head since getting fired. He was eventually able to take all the negative energy behind his anger, and convert it into positive, productive energy that could help power him through his job search.

Anger, in particular, is an emotion that can be destructive to yourself and your search if you allow it to simmer and boil internally. Give it space to breathe by putting it into words - whether verbally to support people in your life, or in writing via journaling. Use your words to turn harmful, negative energy into productive positive progress. Nothing is off the table when articulating anger – just write what you feel without judgement. Also, make sure to leverage your Super Team by seeking people out who will give you honest feedback to the question, "how am I coming across?"

Rewrite Your Self-Talk

Jane willingly moved with her fiancé from Boston to Shreveport where his new job was, but once there, she found herself feeling frustrated and resentful toward him. Because of the move, she had to uproot her life and completely change careers. The decision to move meant leaving a secure job with a company she loved in Boston, with the hopes of landing a new role in account management in Louisiana.

Jane was surrounded by the unknown. Here she was, in this entirely new town, new culture, and admittedly a new pace of life that felt nothing like Boston. She'd also left behind long-time colleagues as well as friends and family. Then came the job search, where she was slapped in the face with rejection after rejection after rejection – no hits on her resumes, no responses to her online applications, and no requests for interviews. She was trying everything and getting nothing in return for her efforts, which only made her even more angry and frustrated.

Not only was she angry at her fiancée, but, as it turned out, she was even angrier at *herself* for going along with the move! On top of that, she was feeling like a failure because of all the rejection in her new job search, she was anxious about starting over in a new career (and potentially failing), and fearful about starting over in a new place where she didn't know anyone.

In a nutshell – Jane was being extremely hard on herself! And the recording of negative thoughts playing in her head wasn't helping her at all.

Once Jane shifted her self-talk through positive affirmations, she felt more confident in getting out, networking, and in doing so, she created positive momentum in her job search. I know this is easier said than done, but the follow through is essential and worth the effort. A shift will happen, and you'll find it is not as difficult as it feels.

Ultimately, Jane's willingness to rewrite her self-talk pushed her outside of her comfort zone, where she forced herself out of the house and went out to meet new people who could help with her job search. Meeting more people, and ultimately friends as well, helped her process the negativity she was feeling about the move so she could open the door to a new positive chapter in her life and her career!

Anger, as we've been discussing, can easily turn into a toxic, progress-thwarting emotion. One of its offshoots can be negative self-talk, which destroys your self-confidence from the inside out. Nip it in the bud by first being aware of any negative thoughts invading your consciousness, and then by using positive affirmations to rewrite it on the spot before it does any damage! Any good therapist will tell you that inner dialogue can be a two-way conversation – you can actually argue with your own negative inner voice as if you were arguing with a friend. It doesn't mean you are crazy, just more at ease in managing your own internal guide voice.

> **Brand Angle: You at Your Best**
>
> **This is the perfect time to remember who you are at your best. Your personal brand can be your "North Star" when the negative self-talk starts going in your head. Thinking about your past career and personal successes can help you begin to rewrite the script to get the positive energy flowing. You can also do this by writing positive affirmations. Positive affirmations are statements that can help you to challenge and overcome negative or self-sabotaging thoughts and they can be based on key parts of your personal brand statement. Take a moment now to write some. For example: "I am a valuable contributor to the company of my dreams - they acknowledge and reward my skills and talents every day!"**

Get The Facts

Matt had a lucrative job as a manager at a large industrial company, where he had quite a bit of authority and prestige that he enjoyed. When looking for a new role following a restructuring, he had plenty of offers, but his biggest challenge was that none of the offers were living up to his expectations financially.

Matt was insulted by the job offers he was receiving. As what he considered lowball offer after offer arrived in his inbox with infuriating, condescending thuds, he got angrier and angrier toward the employers making those offers. He would find what he saw as perfectly logical and factual red flags with each offer, and rule it out on the spot without negotiating. With each offer and each self-imposed veto, Matt's rage increased at his "unfair" situation.

It was clear that behind each red flag and rational justification – was anger. For Matt, the key to getting past his anger enough to see these job offers in a better light, was to focus on the facts of each offer. Once he became aware that his anger was jeopardizing the necessary EQ he'd need to land a promising new job, Matt sat down with a more level head and started researching market pay for the positions he was applying for. He learned he was previously on the very top end of the payscale for his role and level. This is a common realization when someone hears salary offers during a job search.

Armed with the facts and a strategy to negotiate on his own behalf, Matt was then able to adjust his expectations, especially when it came to the salary differentials. He also saw that it might be worth it for his long term career to potentially sacrifice a little bit of salary for the short term.

With his anger abating in the face of these new facts and big picture thinking, Matt revisited some of the offers that he'd initially rejected in anger and discovered that he'd overlooked favorable work cultures, good management and work environments, lucrative benefits, and other positive aspects of the positions.

One offer in particular stood out for Matt and he decided to pursue it. Going over all the details, he felt that the net positive of the offer justified a potential pay cut. As a result, his emotions about it shifted from anger to hope.

At the end of the day though, the employer that Matt decided to attempt to negotiate with, did not budge on their offer and he did not take the job. However, rather than using this negative outcome as a reason to get angry, Matt was able to see it as a positive that he'd made the right decision based on the facts rather than in the heat of anger.

A key takeaway from Matt's story is how he gathered real evidence to support and/or correct the emotion fueled beliefs he had formed around his job search. This tactic reinforces the fact that, despite how it might feel sometimes, a job search is not personal.

Therefore, if you're finding yourself in a resentful space and feel like you are taking rejection personally, do some research and make sure you've got your facts straight. Analyze market pay in your region, assess your value in a position based on education and experience, and look at other aspects of organizations you're applying to, like benefits, culture, and management styles. The more data you have to support your efforts, the stronger your overall position will be in your search. This research will also help you get clear on your core values and what it is you're looking for. It is important that you understand the spectrum of pay scales in your field and where you fell with your last salary. Do not expect a potential employer to know what you made at your last job or to offer a similar salary. Its good business for an employer to save money on salaries, so expect an employer to start with the lowest possible offer.

In a job search, and especially in a negotiation, facts are your friends. Do your homework as early in your search as possible, researching your industry and the market to arm yourself with the right information to use as the foundation of your job search.

Take Control Checkpoint: **Research**

What don't you know about your industry and the job market that could be holding you back? Where can you begin that research today? The internet? Trade publications? Contacting a friend or expert resource to guide you in the right direction? Posting a question on *LinkedIn* to get resource ideas from your network?

Don't Take It Personally

This has been said multiple times already in this chapter, but it bears repeating: Job loss and the job search usually isn't personal, despite how it may feel. The sooner you can get into the mindset that your situation is not personal, the better. It was a business decision. The person hiring is doing so based on criteria that has nothing to do with you, and will hire someone with or without you, so while it may feel personal, you are merely in the crossroads of an empirical process. Another point of view that helps shed how personal it feels is for you to buy into the belief that you do have the skills to take to the open market where you'll be valued. Then you can start taking forward steps in your job search.

Venting

Give yourself sufficient time and space to vent. If you're more of an introvert, "venting" might mean journaling. If you're an extrovert, you might need to seek out people you trust (like your Super Team) and blow off steam verbally to them. Both are right and effective. If the anger you're feeling is too strong to be resolved by those methods, you might consider delaying your job search a bit and giving yourself time to seek an outside resource like a counselor. Feeling stuck by anger is not abnormal and its nothing to fear. With the proper embrace, it is an obstacle you will overcome.

Write A Letter

One way to let your feelings out is to write a letter to your former employer. They will never actually receive this letter because you won't send it. But the practice of writing it - to your old boss, or to the CEO or owner - is a way to make sure you get your feelings out and that they are directed specifically to the person that you hold responsible for your current situation. Read it aloud like you are saying the words to their face. You might even want to yell certain parts of the letter to them! Then you can go through the cathartic process of disposing of the letter. Burn it in your fireplace, or if that isn't an option, you can send it down the garbage disposal. This process is helpful to then let go of the anger. You got it out of your system, so now you can start to move on without the burden of that anger. This is a therapeutic technique that behavioral health professionals deploy frequently when circumstances prevent a direct resolution (such as anger at a family member who has passed away) or when a confrontation isn't advisable. It works beautifully in the job search process.

Personal Coping Strategies

Tap into your self-awareness when you're not in a state of anger and put together a set of strategies that you know will be helpful when you are angry. These could include meditation, prayer, exercise, arts and crafts, listening to certain music, taking a walk outside, more physical activities like boxing, tennis, or martial arts. Exercising while listening to loud music can have a magical effect helping dissipate anger. Finally, never underestimate the emotionally primal but often powerful act of having a good cry.

The key is to know which strategies work for you and lean into them when you need them. We all have emotions and it's important to set aside time to give a voice to them - whether that means introspectively through writing or externally through physical activity. If you don't, they may pop up at the most inopportune moments in your job search. You cannot control what emotions emerge in your life, but you absolutely can control what do about them and how you manage them.

Take Control Checkpoint: **Venting Productively**

What is your MOST effective way to vent anger in a healthy, productive, and safe way?

Physicality

Next time you're feeling angry, take note of your body. For many people, emotions like anger look very contracted, like sitting slumped down in a chair with arms crossed in front of you, fists clenched, chest closed, shoulders hunched up, and head dropped down with your eyes gazing at the ground. Try physically reversing this effect by standing up, unclenching your fists, putting your hands on your hips, opening your chest, putting your shoulders down, lifting up your head, and gazing straight ahead. If you can and the weather allows, go outside, take your shoes and socks off and connect your feet with the earth for a powerful grounding and calming effect. Make a note of how this changes the way your body feels, as well as your emotions, and your self-talk.

Take Control Checkpoint:
Identify the Source & Self-Talk

Ask yourself, "Where is my anger really coming from? Is it still from the initial job loss? Have I fully processed that? Or is it from the current rejections I'm getting in my job search? Am I more angry at other people or myself?" Identify the source of the anger you're currently experiencing.

Next, write down the inner dialogue in your head, especially during the challenging parts of the job search like when you're getting rejections. For example, "I'm not smart enough to get this job."

Then, look at what you've written down, these things you're saying to yourself, and ask: "How is this useful? How is this thinking serving me and my purpose? What can I do differently?"

Key Points:

- Much of the anger felt by job seekers is pent up resentment about the "unfairness" of their situation.

- Self-awareness is critical when it comes to anger, as it can easily seep through to the image you're projecting on the outside.

- As personal as a job loss feels, a key tactic to dealing with anger and moving on, is to realize that it's not personal.

Chapter 5

Fear

A little fear can be a positive motivator in the job search - like a shot of adrenaline to make you perform at your peak level. But in larger quantities it can cripple your best laid plans. Some of the fears triggered by a job loss are based on real threats, like being unable to pay the bills and support yourself and your family. A host of other ones, though, are more perceived than reality.

During the job search process, questions can pop up like - "What if I try to negotiate a job offer and it's rescinded?" Others are far worse, stemming from terrified self-talk, like - "What if I *never* find a job again? Who am I if I'm not working? Are people mocking me behind my back? Will my spouse leave me? Will I lose everything?" A soundtrack like this, played on a daily loop is enough to break the forward momentum of a job search, and more than that - the spirit of the job seeker.

Fear in the job search is a showstopper. It's demotivating, shame inducing, and when it persists, paralyzing. It's also a shape shifter, making it somewhat difficult to spot. Fear quite often shows up as something entirely different.

Assess:
Is fear showing up in your job search?

1. Do you find yourself dreading or avoiding job search activities?
2. Are you withdrawing and isolating yourself from loved ones?
3. Are you experiencing "worst case scenario" thinking or thoughts spiraling out of control?
4. Are you feeling a sense of hopelessness or resignation?
5. Do you have racing or scattered thoughts or the inability to focus or concentrate on tasks?

How Fear Shows Up In The Job Search

Shame

In our achievement based culture, we put so much value on what we do for a living that being out of work can lead to feelings of shame, and being afraid of what people might think of us for being in that situation. For men in particular, fear can show up as feeling too ashamed to admit to others, especially their loved ones, that they've lost their job. In his book *From the Ground Up: My Journey to Reimagine the Role of a Global Business,* Starbucks CEO Howard Schultz recounts the story of a man he encountered every morning at one of the Starbucks stores near the company's corporate offices. When Schultz struck up a conversation with the man, he learned that he'd been unemployed for two months and was showing up at Starbucks every day because he was too afraid to tell his family that he'd lost his job. This man's fear exhibited itself as shame and denial.

Lack Of Focus

Fear can take focus and splinter it into dozens of tiny pieces, like a kaleidoscope does to a light beam. Rather than focusing on your job search with laser-like attention, large amounts of fear send your energy spinning off in random directions, making it difficult or even impossible to get anything done, including critical job search tasks. What may look like irresponsible behavior, in reality, may be fear. With fear, comes lack of focus and faltering commitment.

Anger

Fear also triggers a lack of control, and as human beings, our natural instinct is to *always* be in control. Historically, lack of control over our circumstances could put us in harm's way and threaten our survival. Today, these same primal feelings of fear can show up as an angry, adrenaline-fueled attempt to regain control over a situation where you feel powerless.

Anger stemming from the fear of being powerless often ends up being misdirected at loved ones and sometimes inadvertently in networking situations and worse, job interviews. Unprocessed anger can seep into a job interview faster than you can say "don't call us, we'll call you." A micro facial expression, a change in tone of voice, a quick but biting reference to a prior employer, body language – all these tells and more can make an employer's ears perk up (and not in a good way). Fear may be the emotional root and anger is the symptom, but all the employer on the other side of the table sees is a potential red flag.

Stubbornness

Fear can also show up as stubbornness and resistance to new ideas or change. This might happen, for example, in older job seekers who might already be working from a limiting belief that they're too old to be re-employed. Once laid off, this stubbornness can cause the individual to refuse to learn how job searching in their industry has changed in the years since they last looked for a job.

To others looking on, the person might come off as stubborn, angry, and close-minded. But in reality, their refusal to learn social media strategies is fear in disguise. They're fearful of how the world around them has changed and if there's still a place for them in it. The fear of being irrelevant and easily replaced, can easily turn into anger at the injustice of it all.

Insecurity

It's all but impossible not to feel at least a little insecure about yourself after being told that your services are no longer needed. Being freshly unemployed, submitting resume after resume, application after application and not hearing back, only makes matters worse. Follow that up with a string of less-than-stellar or blown interviews. Now, taking all this into consideration, how do you think your next interview will play out? Will you come off as insecure? If you don't take the time to work through your fears, then the answer is probably yes.

Insecurity is also something that acutely affects immigrants, minorities, and workers who have left the workforce for some time, like stay at home moms. What these individuals have in common is the fear of being rejected based on factors outside of their control. Many carry with them the experience of having been told in the past that they are not qualified for a job they are applying for. This type of insecurity can make an individual so fearful of the job search outcome that they're ready to give up before they start.

> ### *Take Control Checkpoint:* Stop Spinning Up Fear
>
> **Make a list of ALL the reasons you're insecure about your job search. Be brutally honest with yourself because the objective is to get the reasons out of your head and out of your mental spin cycle where all they're doing is spinning up more and more fear. Now make a list at least twice as long of the positives from your personal brand/who you are at your best.**

Procrastination

Similar to insecurity, procrastination can be the reason behind a lack of job search progress at all stages. It can cause you to dawdle on finishing your resume, just to avoid the dreaded interview. Or, on the flip side of procrastination, fear can make you skip critical steps in your search to rush to the interviewing to "get it over with."

Fear can be like stepping into quicksand - the longer and deeper you're in it, the harder it is to get traction to crawl your way out. Like grains of sand, the more fears that accumulate, the harder it is to move. You're not getting things done, and you've fallen off all the time frames you'd set for your job search. Procrastination can be a loud and clear symptom of fear.

Manic Action

Think back to Joe in the introduction. An unemployed executive puts together twenty spreadsheets, ten versions of his elevator pitch and takes networking to a whole new level when he cyberstalks his contacts. This is not just proactive, this is desperation emerging from fear. There is a fine line between a reaction to fear and mental illness, we are addressing the former here.

Fear-driven urgency that drives people to start taking action - any action - is rarely the smartest or most constructive strategy for job searching, or life. Be strategic. If your job search actions resemble an onslaught of any kind, you are likely moving too fast in reaction to fear.

Tactics To Overcome Fear

Get Professional Support

Sheryl was working at her dream job and living in her dream home when the rug was pulled out from under her in the form of a layoff. Unfortunately, this wasn't the first time she had gone through a traumatic job loss. Years before, when she was a single mom with a small child at home, she'd also lost her job and eventually, as a result of the financial strain, she lost her home to foreclosure when she could no longer keep up with the mortgage payments. For a brief time she and her daughter were technically homeless, staying with various friends and family.

Now, in the face of another sudden job loss, Sheryl was terrified. All the emotions from all those years ago (that had never been fully processed) came rushing back with full force, especially the terror any parent feels when faced with the possibility of being unable to protect their child from harm. Sheryl now felt that fear viscerally. Even though her daughter was by now grown and out of the house, she was determined not to be caught by surprise again and have her home taken away from her. So, this time, right after Sheryl was notified that she was laid off, she went home and immediately called her realtor. She put her dream home on the market. Sheryl was kicking off the search for her new job in a state of absolute, crippling fear.

This decision to sell a home when unemployed might very well be the right thing to do. Without the pressure of a mortgage and other bills, it can certainly remove some of the financial and emotional burden. It can provide the space to step back and take a breath while deciding your next move.

But with so much on the line, the most important thing to consider is to not be making critical, life-changing decisions in a state of panic, which is exactly the direction things were going for Sheryl. It was clear that there were some unresolved issues going back to the time she lost her house, so while going down the path of getting the house ready for sale, Sheryl's career coach encouraged her to seek counseling support to fully explore the depths of her fear relating to her current situation. Not surprisingly, the lack of control she had previously drove her to take as much control as possible over her current state of unemployment, even if it came in the heartbreaking form of selling her home.

After thinking through all the considerations, Sheryl became comfortable with the idea of a fresh start in a new home. She was an empty-nester and didn't need all the space, and she eventually became excited about the idea of renting for a while to see where she'd land in her new job so she could buy a smaller home with a shorter commute. For Sheryl, the drastic measure of selling her house turned out to be the right thing for her to do. Key to her coming to this conclusion though, was taking the time to seek professional help to deal with the underlying emotions.

If you suspect that you might need to dig deeper with the guidance of a counsellor or similar health professional, there is no shame in finding a resource to support you on your journey. Dealing with emotions are complicated in the best of circumstances, and with the pressure of a job search, this step might be the key to being able to clear your head and clear the air to find the right path forward.

Own Your Value

Growing up, Devya lived in extreme poverty in India. Life was a daily struggle as her parents tried desperately to provide enough food for her and her siblings. Possibly fueled by her circumstance, as is common in these situations, she grew into a strong, determined young woman, with her eyes set on higher education and moving to America to have a successful career. Devya earned an undergraduate degree in engineering and then moved to the United States to pursue her doctorate. But even though she was already qualified to work in engineering, the only jobs she felt confident enough to apply for were restaurant server positions. As a female immigrant, the idea of competing with American engineers for a job in her chosen field was simply too scary to Devya. This fear of rejection kept her locked in the limiting belief that if she kept working within the safe confines of waiting tables at restaurants, she wouldn't have to worry about being turned down for jobs in her field.

In addition to her choice to pursue "safety jobs" in restaurants, Devya's fear-driven lack of self-confidence was also reflected in her overly humble resume. It was far too succinct for someone of her impressive academic background. Her resume was simply a list of brief, blunt statements and bullet points, but without elaboration or really any attempt to "sell" potential employers on her true value as an employee in the field of engineering. Fear was clearly in the driver's seat of Devya's job search, blocking her from seeing all she had to offer to her industry.

With a new focus on branding, she was able to build awareness about her lack of self-confidence. Devya then rewrote her resume, expanding on what had once been succinct, less than attention grabbing bullet points. She now began to see herself in a new, more positive light. Her fears of not being good enough or as qualified as American engineers slowly melted away. Her confidence started coming back as she remembered all she'd gone through in her life to get to this point. Devya soon felt brave enough to start applying for jobs in the engineering field, where her knowledge and passion clearly lived. Once fear was no longer in her way, Devya was able to take herself and her passions seriously.

Within a short time, she was offered a fantastic position as a network systems engineer at a large organization and joyfully quit her restaurant job. Once she overcame her old fears and the self-talk that she didn't matter, she began believing she was worth more than a "safety job," and it was true!

No matter which emotion you are struggling with, and where you are in your search, focusing on your personal brand - who you are at your best - and making this clear through your resume, LinkedIn, and brand statement, is one of the single most emotionally uplifting tactics you can execute during your job search. Reviewing your resume with fresh eyes to align it with your personal brand and ensuring that your accomplishments stand out takes a relatively small amount of time and can yield great dividends that help you own your value.

Leap Of Faith

Katherine didn't exactly hate her job, working as a customer service coordinator at a utilities company. But she didn't love it either. It didn't give her that often indescribable "spark" the people get when they have a real passion for their career.

That's why when her department was downsized and she was laid off, she was briefly optimistic about the opportunity to take her career in a different direction. But once she confronted her bank account and the reality that the search for a job in a new field could possibly outlast her available funds, fear set in. Fear in the form of dread that the only reasonable decision was to find a job as quickly as possible, which almost certainly meant that it would be similar to her old job. She was scared to explore something completely different, but Katherine felt the walls closing in around her as she contemplated the idea of going right back into the box from which she had just been freed. She wondered if there was a way to merge making a living doing something she loved. But first, she'd need to find out what that even was.

What Katherine did know in her heart, beyond a shadow of a doubt, was that her passion was working with animals. She'd grown up on a farm, taking care of all sorts of farm and domesticated animals. Her family called her 'the animal whisperer' for her ability to calm the animals when they were upset and understand their needs.

Once she admitted out loud what she really wanted to do for a living, she was able to open herself up to the possibility of doing it. She began researching potential opportunities to work with animals. Even as she did the tactical work and research, Katherine still could not fathom that she'd be able to make a living doing something she loved so much. It seemed more like a pipe dream to her especially after working for so long in a job that did nothing more than pay the bills. But to her credit, even though her emotions and limiting beliefs were doing their best to hamstring her, Katherine plowed forward with the tactical pieces of this potential career shift: research and networking with people in different organizations that had a connection with animals. Moving forward in her job search every day helped turn her limiting beliefs into constructive action.

Ultimately, she decided to take a leap of faith and pursue her passion for working with animals. In doing so, her fears about not being able to earn a living *and* be happy, dissolved, and Katherine landed a great job at The Humane Society. The pay was a step back from what she had previously been earning, and in many ways she was starting from square one in a new career in the nonprofit space. But for Katherine, the fact that she was able to do something she loved for a living, more than made up for it!

Visualization

Don't let the associations with the "self-help/new age" world fool you. Visualization is an extremely powerful tool in fighting fear in the job search, especially in the most commonly feared stage: interviewing. The more specificity you can include in your visualization the better. Walk your mind through the entire process of the job interview, from the moment you wake up in the morning, all the way to walking in the door, shaking the interviewer's hand, through the interview, go into detail on your responses to questions based on your preparation, to walking out of the building afterward, head held high, feeling completely confident about the experience that has just unfolded. Picture what you'll wear down to the most minute details like shoes and jewelry, how you'll answer each question, and imagine feeling calm yet energized during the entire interview. Now visualize the smiles of approval from the interviewer - let no detail go unnoticed.

Go through this visualization as many times as you need until you feel the fear associated with the interview, begin to subside. Practice dealing with your fears now, during your visualization, so your body and mind will have memorized how to respond during the actual event.

Interviewing Fears

Insecurity can impede job search progress at all stages, especially during interviewing and networking. These are the most "social" phases of looking for a job. In the western culture we have specific expectations around an interview, including that a strong applicant should interview well. This isn't always the case of course. There are many talented, skilled individuals who would excel in the job itself, but they just don't interview well.

Add to those expectations, the insecurity of a recent (or not so recent) job loss, and the fear generated by a job interview can be downright crippling. This fear of a bad job interview can paralyze many individuals early in the job search, well before the interview stage, making them come off as insecure in something as basic as a networking email or phone call.

Mock interviewing is a tactic any job seeker can deploy to dissolve fears around interviewing, whether you have a coach or not. Enlist the help of your spouse, family member, or friend and give them a list of standard job interview questions (if you're at a loss - simply google interview questions related to your role or level!). If possible, perform this multiple times, in multiple mediums - in person, over the phone and virtually via webcam, since that's how many job interviews these days are done. In addition to providing you feedback on how you answer the questions and how you come across overall, also ask them to weigh in on how you're dressed, lighting, backdrop and anything else they notice that an interviewer might key in on as well.

The key to success with this tactic is repetition. Practice, practice, practice! Do as many mock/virtual job interviews as needed until you feel prepared and confident.

Take Control Checkpoint: Mock Interview List

Make a list of all the people you could ask to do mock interviews with you - friends, family, former colleagues, coaches, and business contacts. Pick one person on your list, reach out to them, and schedule a mock interview with them. Because you want this to be objective, do not pick someone with unfinished or complicated emotional entanglements such as an ex-girlfriend/boyfriend.

> **Brand Angle: "Tell me about yourself."**
>
> **One of the oldest, most common, and seemingly easiest interview questions is also the one that makes many applicants the most fearful: "Tell me about yourself." Why should this be when this question is simply asking for your personal brand statement? If you've done your personal brand work, feel confident in your personal brand, and spend some time aligning your statement to each role you're applying for, rather than creating fear, this standard interview question can generate excitement! As an applicant, this is your opportunity to set the tone for the interview - to let the interviewer know, "Wow, this is a really interesting person with excellent capabilities relevant to this role, and this conversation is going to be great!"**

"How Old Is That Fear?"

When assessing and processing each of your job search fears, ask yourself this question, and journal about what comes up. At what age do you first recall any variation of this current fear? For example, if you're afraid of job interviewing, maybe you trace it back to a humiliating public speaking incident at age 12, making the answer to "how old is that fear?" - "12 years old." Once you've made that connection, you'll have gained the awareness (a very powerful tool in itself!) to separate out your 12-year-old public speaking fear with your current adult interviewing fear and work from there. (It's important to note that if your childhood fear stems from a more serious incident and is disrupting your adult life beyond your job search, I would urge you to please seek out professional help.)

Imagine (And Plan For) The Worst Case Scenario

First - name your worst fear pertaining to your job loss. For some, simply stating your fear out loud will be enough. Saying the words out loud could be enough to make you realize that your worst fear will most likely not come true.

But if that's not the case, the next step is to picture the worst possible thing that could happen if that fear became reality. What would be the most devastating thing that could happen if this fear came true? Imagine how you would feel, physically and mentally. Make the vision as real and detailed as possible.

Now plan in concrete terms what you would do, and how you would respond if this thing actually happened. How would you take care of yourself and your loved ones? How would you carry on? Once you have your plan in place, accept this worst case scenario as a possibility. Then acknowledge that you are prepared to deal with it. You can also create a plan to do everything possible to keep this scenario from happening. Finally, release this "worst case" fear with gratitude for the lessons and preparation it has brought and shift your attention back to more positive, desirable outcomes to your situation.

This tactic has been particularly helpful to me during challenging business situations. While significant fears probably won't just fade away completely, realizing that the worst case scenario is still manageable allowed me to stop being paralyzed by fear and start to move forward.

"Where's The Evidence?"

When it comes to busting some of those "worst case scenario" fears, one quick and actionable fear busting technique is to ask the question - "Where's the evidence?" What actual data is there that has caused you to come to the conclusion that this awful thing is certain to happen? Our minds, especially when gripped with a strong emotion like fear, are highly irrational. Pull out of the emotional spiral by identifying what's real versus what your mind has conjured up as such.

Forcing yourself to seek evidence will uncover some of the limiting beliefs, gremlin voices, and self-doubts that are feeding your fears. Remember that even though it might hit us where it hurts - money, dignity, sense of self, and professional identity - a job loss is not personal, despite what your emotions would have you believe.

Networking Fears

Fear of networking, especially in introverted individuals, can lead to hiding behind a computer all day, relying on technology to do the work and hopefully land them a job. Unfortunately, during the initial round of applying for a job, the only thing clicking "send" connects them with, is an AI driven sorting system in HR that reviews their information (along with the hundreds or thousands of other technically qualified applicants for the job) and automatically makes the decision as to who gets to move on to the next round. But computer algorithms aren't the ones making final hiring decisions - hiring managers are. Networking creates the best odds at connecting with those managers and getting noticed. In fact, the Little Gray Book of Recruiting Benchmarks study performed by Lever, a recruitment marketing firm, shows that candidates referred internally by employees are almost ten times more likely to be hired than people who simply apply online. Now *there* is a reason to invest in your networking strategy!

When you identify a job that you're interested in, it's up to you to network your way to the hiring manager of that position. This might mean doing some reconnaissance via your *LinkedIn* network, former colleagues, your friends and family, or other social media networks. The goal is to strip away the layers of connections between you and that hiring manager, one "known" contact at a time. Begin by initiating casual conversation with the people you know the most who have connections to your target - the hiring manager (or at least other people that work at that company). Then, ask those people for introductions to people in the "inner layers" closer to your target, start conversations with those people and so on.

Find the ten or so jobs that really interest you and work your way, connection by connection, to the hiring manager of each position. The facts are clear that this is a far more effective strategy than blindly sending applications and form emails for 100 different jobs with no personal contacts. It's a rifle approach versus a shotgun - you're much more likely to hit the target.

If the idea of all those personal conversations is daunting, remember - start with the people you know. Start with a friendly, casual conversation like this: "Hello? How have you been? I wanted to let you know that I'm interested in applying for a job at company X and I noticed you used to work there (or you know people there). I would love to have a conversation and get your input if possible." Remember also that networking is a two-way street so don't forget to ask each person what *they're* looking for and how you can help *them*. Then - work from there. Focus on one human conversation at a time - connect, ask for their input, and ask how you can be of service to them.

Another tactic to help with networking fears is to put yourself in the shoes of the person you're reaching out to. How would you feel if a former colleague or acquaintance from church asked for your help? Chances are you'd probably be more than happy to be of service! Most people actually want to be helpful. Most of the time, the fear of reaching out is built up in our head to be much more extreme than it needs to be!

Take Control Checkpoint: Networking Plan

Create your networking plan - where will you network, how often, which events do you need to put on your calendar? Put an upcoming networking event in your area on your calendar right now and create a goal for what you want to get out of each event you attend.

Key Points:

- Fear comes in many disguises including anger, stubbornness, anti-social behavior, flaky or manic behavior and more. Be open to consider if the root cause of some of these other feelings or behaviors might indeed be fear.

- Central to the majority of fear processing tactics is being willing to get past its many masks and determine the root of the fear.

- Interviewing and networking are common fears in job search. The key tactic for both, is practice, practice, practice!

Part III

Paralyzing Emotions

"Next time you're feeling perplexed as to why you're not getting traction on your job search, why not stand on the shoulders of giants so you can land your ideal job faster? Your network, friends, family all want to help. Find the help that best fits you so your job search doesn't have to be lonely."
-Michelle Robin

Chapter 6

Denial

A number of years ago, my mom was diagnosed with breast cancer. I had always seen her as such a strong and capable woman that the idea of her succumbing to cancer was nearly incomprehensible to me. I think it was incomprehensible to her too. She plowed through with work, didn't tell anyone outside of her closest friends and family, and kept moving forward business as usual.

We were both living in our own worlds of denial when she was first diagnosed. I couldn't handle the idea of a world without her, and she thought if she just kept pushing forward, she could outrun the threat of the cancer. Well, we were blessed that she persevered and kicked cancer's butt, not only once, but a second time ten years later. We both handled things differently the second time around. I made sure to be much more attentive to her and be more present with her treatments, and she was much more open and welcomed the broad support of friends and family.

In this case, the denial of the first bout with cancer yielded a successful result. Denial served its purpose, but it left both of us with regrets. When given the opportunity to relive the experience, we both decided to embrace the uncertainty and be more vulnerable. Denial works as a coping mechanism. Until it doesn't. It's a matter of knowing when you must move past the denial phase and move forward.

The same applies when you've just lost your job or received a rejection in your job search. If it feels most natural for you to go back to your computer and start sending out even more resumes and applications as a way of dealing with the loss, so be it. As long as you don't compromise on the quality of your resumes and applications (make sure you're not sending out materials with mistakes), that's fine. Also, at some point, revisit the situation and assess what you could improve on moving forward. After you've taken those two steps though - it's time to move on. Is denial currently showing up for you as you search for your next job?

Assess:
Is denial showing up in your job search?

1. **Are you avoiding talking about, or minimizing ("I'll be fine ...") being laid off or in transition especially with loved ones?**
2. **Are you rationalizing why you're in transition or why you can't find your next role, including blaming others?**
3. **Do you find yourself making excuses for not following through on something?**
4. **Are you spending money and maintaining the same lifestyle despite the loss of income?**
5. **Are you relying on your *perception* of your efforts ("I must have applied to 100 jobs so far and talked to 50 people today!") versus actually *measuring* your job search efforts (10 applications submitted, 3 networking contacts made)?**

How Denial Shows Up In The Job Search

Denial can be an important part of the grieving process. A brief overview of Elisabeth Kubler-Ross's stages of grief shows denial as the first stage, followed by anger, bargaining, depression, and acceptance. The reality of moving through grief is, of course, more complicated and certainly less linear than that. But the basic concept holds true, that denial often shows up as a natural component of grief.

But like an expert poker player, denial rarely shows its hand. Instead, a person in denial about their job loss may show up as overconfident, hyperactive, or what others might perceive as "lazy" - refusing to lift a finger toward getting a new job. If you're seeing yourself in any of these signs, read on.

Hypomania

Fran's sudden layoff came as such a shock, her immediate thought was to whip up a cover letter and resume and send it off ASAP to as many companies as she could Google - and fast. Unfortunately "fast" is not usually synonymous with "good" and Fran's documents reflected it. Her letters and resume were full of typos, sloppy formatting, and overall, presented a less-than-stellar reflection of the personal brand she wished to showcase. The problem was, by the time she realized it, the damage had been done. Once you hit send, no matter what your personal circumstances are, or what's happening emotionally that is influencing your actions, there are no do overs.

Denial of the pain of job loss can launch an individual into what some might call "manic" action specifically "hypomania." This state is characterized by decreased sleep and rest, and increased energy, talking, confidence and bursts of creative ideas. It's busy for the sake of being busy, rushing forward as quickly as possible to avoid dealing with difficult emotions.

Hypomania can mean diving into the physical tasks of the job search without first taking a breath and creating space to process the reality of the job loss. Denial in the job search can result in sending out a sloppily written resume for the sake of speed, incomplete job applications, and hyperactive interviews full of fast talking, interrupting the interviewer, and blurting things out inappropriately (possibly about your former employer). It's motion for the sake of motion, with minimal mindfulness, all to deny the emotions bubbling up. Hypomania is ready, fire, aim.

> ### *Take Control Checkpoint:*
> ### Review Your Application
>
> **Give a second look to the examples of denial in the job search above - sloppily written resume, incomplete applications, and unproductive interview behavior. Take some time now to review your application materials, if for nothing else than peace of mind. (As for the interview behavior, get feedback with a mock interview or simply add it to your radar as something to check yourself for before future interviews.) Reach out to your Super Team for feedback on all of the above as well!**

Perpetual Motion

Similar to hypomania but minus the emotional "manic" component, perpetual motion is exactly what it sounds like - moving for the sake of movement. It's playing a job search numbers game, mainly to convince yourself and others that you're doing "something." It's clicking send on hundreds of identical job applications, or sending formulaic direct messages to dozens of social media contacts, all to convince yourself that you're doing everything you can, so if you're not getting results it's not your fault.

Denying what it actually requires to be successful means turning a blind eye to job search best practices, opting instead for the path of least resistance - constant motion but with no real substance behind it. This tends to happen early in the job search, during the period of emotional turbulence following the loss but can show up in all stages. Later in the loss, perpetual motion can arise from a place of emotional numbness, as you begin to feel beaten down and overwhelmed by the whole process. In both cases, movement masks dealing honestly with your feelings.

Inaction

Another shade of emotional numbness, at the other end of the spectrum from hyperactivity, is complete inaction. In some cases, the grief from a job loss combined with the overwhelming number of steps required to look for a new one, may cause you to simply shut down. On the surface, people around you might wonder if you even *want* a new job. You might find yourself coming up with individual rationalizations for avoiding each job search action, from rewriting your resume, to researching job opportunities, to submitting applications, and networking.

Or sometimes, instead of rationalizations, you might feel embarrassment or shame at your inability to keep moving forward (sometimes hidden in substance use or other forms of escapism). Inaction might happen early in the search or, more often than not, later on, when rejections have piled up and it's hard to see any sort of light at the end of the tunnel.

Tactics To Overcome Denial

Lean On Your Super Team

Shame that comes from a job loss can lead to tight-lipped silence, as the individual chooses to deny their situation as a way of protecting their loved ones from worry. They might be feeling scared, betrayed or embarrassed. Silence is the path of least resistance around those denial-based feelings. As a result, they keep their unemployment a secret, especially from those they love the most.

Mark had been unemployed for four months, but he didn't tell his wife. He'd get up and go through the motions of going to his job as a city bus driver every day at the usual time, but then go sit at a coffee shop or sometimes wander aimlessly about during the day. He'd then return home at the usual time, acting as if he'd been at work all day. He didn't want his wife to worry about him.

But when Mark revealed his secret to some trusted friends in his church group, they pointed out that because of the fairly obvious change in his behavior and emotional state, his wife was probably already a nervous wreck worrying about the cause of these sudden changes in her husband. And the way the human mind works (especially the female human mind I can say firsthand), without knowing the reason for her husband's changed behavior, she had likely already dreamed up a scenario far worse than job loss.

Bingo! When Mark finally summoned the courage to come clean with his wife, she burst into tears – not of sadness but of *relief.* She thought he was having an affair! Now it was Mark's turn to burst into tears. The floodgates opened and, after four months, he was finally able to begin processing his grief from losing his job in a healthy way, rather than hiding it. Mark's shame over being unemployed ended up manifesting in keeping it secret from his wife. But once he spoke those words out loud to his Super Team of friends in his church group, he realized he would need to summon the courage to tell his wife the truth if he had any hope of moving his – and their – life forward.

Denial is nearly always a symptom of a greater pain, in this case shame. Once you're able to uncover that truth, you'll be positioned to address it at its core and move through it. There is also a strong lesson here about not going it alone. You might be able to process some aspects of these emotions by yourself, but most require some level of support, whether from a spouse, or other loved one, a close friend, or even an outside coach or professional. If you find that denial is holding you back from admitting you need help, find the courage to lean on your Super Team. There's no need to suffer in silence.

Take Control Checkpoint: **Super Team Roll Call**

Who are the members of YOUR Super Team? Write their names down and then let each person know that they're on your team and how they can help you during your job search.

Reality Check

While confidence is a positive characteristic in the job search, overconfidence can shoot you in the foot. Denial-fueled overconfidence comes from intentionally focusing on how you think your job search *should* turn out versus how it's *actually* unfolding. For instance, taking a "know it all" approach with a potential employer because you believe you're worth more than the salary being offered, (but with no data to back up this assessment), can potentially sabotage an offer negotiation. Or in some cases, overconfidence means downplaying the potentially negative consequences of a job loss, particularly financial ones, believing that a new job is just around the corner, when the reality of the situation is quite different.

Depending on the state of the economy and your function, industry, education, and geographical preferences it can take a month to find a job for every $10,000 of the paycheck you would like to earn. So, in theory, if you were looking to earn $60,000 a year, your job search could take approximately six months. This is not a completely linear equation. It's a rule of thumb for estimation purposes so please do not calculate and get discouraged. The point is not to underestimate that searches can take time, especially with more senior positions.

When Joe, a sales executive, was laid off, he didn't panic. In fact, he saw the situation as no big deal, absolutely believing that he would send out a few resumes and *bam* - awesome new job! He felt he was "eminently qualified" for any position he sought. Denying the reality and potential length of a job search, he enthusiastically jumped into his search, buoyed by his beliefs that his resume was stellar, he was great at interviewing, and his networking skills were top notch.

It was a slap in the face for Joe when potential employers (as evidenced by his lack of interviews) did not seem to see him as he saw himself. Finally, as his job search dragged on from weeks to months, Joe slowly emerged from denial and faced the reality of his situation. He became open to using job search tools that he had previously rejected, like mock interviewing, so he'd be able to see for himself what interviewers saw. Once he saw the gap between perception and reality, the wheels shifted in his mind and he began actively practicing and sharpening his interview skills, recording and analyzing video recorded interviews until he was finally satisfied with what he saw on camera.

It took Joe longer than he initially anticipated to land a new job - months rather than weeks. Key to his success was his willingness to take an honest look at the actual impression he was making on employers rather than the one he thought he was conveying. This is a great lesson in using self-awareness to close the gap between the personal brand you think is on display versus the one that really is.

Joe also carried over this attitude of self-improvement into a day-to-day Job Search Action Plan. This day-to-day plan contains specific actions that you can take continuously to move your job search forward. Keep it in a notebook, a Word document, spreadsheet, project management application or otherwise, as long as it keeps you moving forward, one step at a time. The most successful tool will be the one that you check in with and use daily.

Take Control Checkpoint:
Job Search Action Plan Tasks.

1. Get clear about your job search goals (what you want to do in terms of role, field or industry, type of company, such as Fortune 500 vs. small business, geography, level that you'll find acceptable, financial requirements, etc.)

2. Get crystal clear on your personal brand. Who are you at your best? What unique value will you bring to an employer?

3. Set a deadline for writing/editing your Resume/CV and LinkedIn profile.

4. Research the jobs in your industry and the labor market for your industry and geography.

5. Generate a list of target companies you'd like to work for. Internet searches might be a good place to start for this, as well as LinkedIn. Your local library/librarian can even help you narrow this down!

6. Create your social media plan - which networks will you use (presumably mainly but not exclusively LinkedIn), what time(s) of day will you go on them and for which specific tasks (to avoid mindlessly scrolling through your feeds)?

7. Develop a networking event plan - where you will search for events, how often you'd like to attend events, and your plan of action for each one (Will you need business cards? How many? Have you prepared your elevator pitch?).

8. Meet with at least one person every week that has a direct connection to someone at one of your target companies.

9. Approach friends and other trusted contacts about scheduling mock/virtual interviews to hone your interviewing skills and presence.

Note: This is by no means an exhaustive list of items for your job search action plan. This could be (and is!) the subject matter of a book all on its own. If you feel you need to explore more in this area, there are many great books, websites and career coaches that can point you in the right direction. This list is meant to point you in the right direction to make sure you're focusing on the right things in your search.

Diversify Your Strategy And Seek Tough Love

To Alexa, her layoff at a large global chemical company didn't feel like a job loss. Even though her current position was no longer available, she was told that the company was still hiring in other areas. Alexa loved working at that company, so she began applying to jobs in other divisions of the same company that had just let her go - but only to those jobs. She did not seek a single opportunity outside of the company.

Alexa was in denial about being "actually" unemployed and therefore did not engage in a full job search. She was hoping, on some level, that if she was picked up by another division, her life wouldn't have to change much because the piece of her identity that was attached to being an employee of this company and this culture, would remain intact. Due to a combination of denial and fear of the unknown, Alexa was sabotaging her ultimate job search success by choosing to play small.

When challenged about this by her career coach, Alexa eventually was able to move out of denial about wanting to stay with the organization that had just let her go. She expanded her vision to outside employers, and Alexa was able to move forward in her search with greater intention. She subsequently landed a job that she was very optimistic about and began reshaping that piece of her identity around her new company, freeing it from the shackles of her old one.

What can we learn from Alexa's story? A few things. First, it's important to diversify your job search strategy. Don't put all your eggs in one basket thereby drastically limiting your options.

Next, ask yourself: Are you looking at your situation realistically? Or is the lens of your thinking clouded by emotion, especially if you were laid off recently? One way to tell is by looking for actual hard evidence to back up your beliefs about your situation. In Alexa's case, she wasn't getting the results she was hoping for with her narrow search, which she was finally able to see when challenged by her Super Team. Her former employer was not as loyal to her as she was to them, and this needed to be recognized.

Don't be afraid to seek out tough love. Alexa used her coach for this purpose but you could also turn to your Super Team - friends and family members whom you trust to have your best interests in mind and tell you constructive truths that will move you out of denial and back into the game.

Dig Deep

When you say something out loud or write it down, it sounds a lot less scary than when it's bouncing around in your head. As always, journaling is an extremely effective activity for processing emotions like denial, allowing you to get the thoughts in your head onto the page where they're almost always less confusing and overwhelming.

Start with an all-purpose brain dump, and from there, begin asking yourself probing questions (like those in the self-assessment checklist at the beginning of this chapter) to bring your situation into focus. Identify any irrational beliefs you're holding about your situation (for example: being unemployed means your loved ones are looking down on you, or if you don't find a job quickly you might end up homeless, etc.).

The act of journaling, freeing your thoughts from your head onto the page, will help slow down the events happening around you, see the big picture more objectively and intellectually, and move you out of emotional overwhelm. Remember, your journal is for your eyes only, so you can be totally honest with yourself! Getting clear on what's actually happening and how you feel about it, will also give you the confidence to move forward and take intentional action in your job search.

Celebrate Your Wins

Like anything that matters in life, a successful job search is a marathon, not a sprint. Celebrating your wins, no matter how small, and doing it consistently, creates positive momentum tactically *and* emotionally, getting you "unstuck" from emotions that aren't moving you forward.

For instance, a friend was feeling down on herself for blowing a final interview. Stuck in tunnel vision, all she could focus on was that one failed interview. Once she zoomed out, however, she saw the three successful rounds of interviews that got her that final interview in the first place.

Zooming out further, she was able to focus on the fact that she was still a finalist for two remaining opportunities. With that perspective, she was finally able to take a moment and celebrate how far she'd come in her search. Once she successfully separated this temporary negative outcome from all the positive possibilities that were still lined up, her perspective shifted and her entire process was reenergized.

These moments of personal celebration and self-acknowledgement can also act as rest stops – places to breathe and reboot and refocus along the way, especially in a longer, drawn out job search. There are no wins too small for acknowledgment!

Key Points:

- **A common symptom of denial is often frenzied "movement for the sake of movement" vs. more goal directed, intentional, strategic job search actions.**

- **As much as you might want to hide from the world and not tell anyone about your job loss, one of the healthiest and most productive things you can do right now is to open up to others - whether your spouse, loved ones, or members of your Super Team.**

- **Creating an Action Plan with specific, measurable, daily and weekly action items and due dates is also a valuable tactic for working through any feelings of denial. Limiting the Action Plan to small measurable steps will help overcome the obstacle denial presents and keep it from persisting.**

Chapter 7

Frustration

Lack of control can make anyone feel helpless. In the job search process, going on interview after interview, getting zero feedback, no offers, and sending application after application into what seems like an electronic black hole, can become an extremely frustrating experience. Being cut off from direct access to hiring managers and decision makers only makes things worse. It can truly seem like your career and your future are at the mercy of a nameless, faceless system. Over time, the resulting feelings of helplessness and acute frustration can build.

Frustration is like that innocent little chip in your car windshield. At first you don't think anything of it because it's not impeding your vision or your ability to drive. Then, the chip becomes a thin hairline fracture right down the center of your windshield. It's distracting, but you can still see and the car still works. It's the sudden temperature change, however, that finally brings the crack to its breaking point, creating a spider web of glass fractures that spread throughout your windshield making your car undrivable.

Frustration when ignored, can have serious if not unintended consequences. Just like the glass fracture, if left unchecked it can lead to a downward spiral of other destructive emotions. It might start small but once it grows, it is just as serious as all the other loss emotions (grief, anger and fear) paralyzing emotions (denial, anxiety and loneliness).

If you sit in frustration day after day without attempting to address it, you could taint your overall brand impression. The frustration you're feeling with the job search might be throwing off negative cues not only in interviews but also in networking situations. The longer you try to ignore it, the worse it's bound to get, and the more people are bound to notice.

Assess:
Is frustration showing up in your job search?

1. **Have you set realistic expectations and clear goals for your search?**
2. **Do you feel paralyzed from indecision about the next best step to take to move forward in your job search?**
3. **Do you feel overwhelmed when thinking about or engaging in job search actions?**
4. **Do you find yourself aiming for "perfect," hearing yourself saying things like "nothing is right" and "nothing is good enough"?**
5. **Are you finding only negatives in how well your job search is going overall?**

How Frustration Shows Up In The Job Search

Inaction

Many times, frustration in the job search can come from feeling like you're spinning your wheels in place and not getting anywhere, especially when you're newly unemployed. Frustrated and overwhelmed by your often unexpected new situation, you might freeze, unable to see the next step forward. All the things your logical brain "knows" you should be doing - resume, personal brand statement, networking, etc. - seem trapped behind a wall of fog, unreachable. In the context of "fight, flight or freeze" - the frustration you are feeling about being suddenly unemployed, often makes you freeze.

Inaction can show up as freezing like this, stuck in analysis paralysis, unable to decide what to do next. It can also show up later in the job search, after you've been grinding away day after day and not seeing results. After investing in all that effort without seeing results, it's understandable if you throw your hands up in the air as if to say, "Why even bother?"

Behavior Changes

Before her sudden layoff, Paula was as reliable as they come. Her word was her bond, so if she said she would be somewhere, she'd be there early. She was never the type to reschedule important appointments, cancel at the last minute, or blow off even the most casual social engagements. Nowadays though, she was doing all these things and regularly. Without realizing it, Paula had become the type of person she used to shake her head in disbelief at: a "total flake." When she did buckle down and focus on her job search, her actions were half-hearted and sloppy - like sending out her old resume by mistake. Her family and old friends were in shock - this was *not* the person they knew! When they questioned her, Paula dodged and deflected their questions, always changing the subject to something less threatening.

On the inside of this bizarre bubble of new behavior, Paula was feeling down on herself and stuck in frustration. She was frustrated at being unemployed, at not knowing what to do next, and at having her previously organized, predictable, peaceful life jerked into confusion and chaos. She was frustrated most of all by being unable to "snap out of it." Frustration made things that used to be second nature – time management, basic organization, and attention to detail – feel like the most tedious chores.

Paula's story highlights someone acting contrary to their standard behavior, in this case, showing signs of "flakiness" observable by others. This is just one example of many behavior changes that can occur in the face of frustration in the job search. Sudden or dramatic behavior changes can be your emotionally stressed mind's way of saying, "I can't deal with this!" The important thing is to realize this is reactionary and it's not who you have become, it's not permanent regression, and that old efficient you that was always on the ball is still there.

Take Control Checkpoint: **Behavior Changes**

Have you noticed any sudden or dramatic behavioral changes since losing your job? Things that have stood out in your mind and made you think, "That's not me!" Perhaps others have mentioned something to you along these lines. Take a moment to acknowledge these behavior changes, exercise a little self-compassion and then explore if it might be frustration triggering the behavior changes.

Tactics To Overcome Frustration

High Value Activities

Erin, an operations manager, could tell you with pinpoint accuracy the source of *her* frustration: she was wrongfully let go. Through her eyes, the way her termination was handled was completely botched. It seemed to come out of the blue and she remembered something being said in the exit conversation about her "not knowing enough about industry changes," which she interpreted in the heat of the moment as being called "dumb".

The frustration she was feeling about being fired for something she felt was out of her control was also mixed with anger and fear about her future. Mixed together, this storm of emotions was paralyzing her and keeping her from moving forward in the hunt for her next job. A week after hearing the news and still stewing about the injustice of being fired, Erin still had not kicked off her job search. She was treading water and letting her emotions get the best of her.

Normally, Erin was a very direct, task oriented, hard working individual. Those characteristics came up time and time again on every personality assessment she'd ever taken and in better times, she used them to her advantage to climb the corporate ladder. What she needed now was a way to redirect those strengths into her job search and to do it in a purposeful, strategic way rather than motion for the sake of motion, which would keep her treading water and feeling frustrated.

She drafted a job search action plan, and key to this plan was getting clear on her most high value activities. The most productive actions that would in turn then create the most momentum in her job search. The alternative is spending forty hours a week doing a whole bunch of smaller things that filled time, but did not get her closer to landing a job. One of those actions was based on Erin's goal to rapidly advance her knowledge about the latest developments and skills in her field. Now thinking more clearly and less emotionally, she was able to acknowledge the feedback she received when she was let go. To that end, she developed a list of weekly reading assignments of various industry trade journals, blogs, and other articles that supported her learning goals. The list and the checkmarks on it showing she completed the various tasks served as an accountability tool for Erin. It wasn't long before the frustration she'd felt in part from being fired for something "beyond her control" had abated. That was when the rest of her job search gained real momentum, and within a month she was reviewing promising job offers!

At the root of frustration is often an inability to decide what to do next with the amount (or perceived amount) of options in front of you. This is when it's helpful to ask yourself: What is the SINGLE most valuable action I can take right now to move my job search forward? Think of the Pareto Principle, also known as the "80/20 rule" - where 20% of your actions will produce 80% of your results. This idea simply means a small number of actions have a much larger impact than others and therefore require focus and priority. Do an honest analysis matching up your actions to your outcomes, identify the 20% of activities creating the most and best results, and ensure they are central to your job action plan!

> ### *Take Control Checkpoint:* 80/20 Action Plan
>
> **Do the "80/20" analysis described above. Are you spending your time on "high value activities"? Hint: this usually looks like actively networking your way into specific openings/companies, working on your personal brand, preparing for interviews (depending on which part of the job search you're in), or things specific to your search like the example above. Searching job boards is NOT a "high value activity." Most importantly, ACT on the results of your analysis and make the appropriate changes to your schedule!**

Energy Management

Todd, a new grad out of Stanford, was a high energy, super ambitious guy by nature. He always seemed to be triple scheduled, overbooked, and running in a million different directions, at work and in his personal life. All through college he had two jobs, was always in a relationship (or two!), worked out religiously, was active leading volunteer activities, and participated in community activities.

Therefore, upon graduation, when it was time to commence the search for a long-term job, at the threshold of a career, Todd found it difficult to slow down and concentrate his attention on his job search. He had too many irons in the fire and was simply stretching his time and energy in too many different directions to make a productive impact on his action plan.

This is where we introduced Todd to three key tactics to help him better focus his attention: priority management, energy management, and activity tradeoffs. The first step was a time tracking tool where he would input hour by hour, on a daily basis, where he was investing his time, especially the biggest chunks or "rocks" of time. At the end of each day he would then review the "big rocks" of time and assess which ones required the most energy and where they fell in the sequence of his day.

He made the immediate observation that most of the activities requiring the greatest amount of his mental and physical energy were grouped together in the first half of his day. By the time he got home to settle in and work on his job search, he was out of juice and that affected the quality of his actions and his results. This left him feeling frustrated about his career not moving forward like he thought it would, but not knowing what to do about it. In his mind, his time commitments were all required, not optional. In college, no matter how busy he was, he had always found a way to "make it work" even flying by the seat of his pants, pulling caffeine-fueled "all-nighters" as needed. The problem was, this strategy did not supply him with the sustained mental and physical energy required to effectively launch a meaningful career.

Todd's frustration opened the door to a conversation about activity tradeoffs he could make in order to pull focus back to his job search. Maybe he didn't "need" to work out for two hours every morning, or he could do an hour in the morning and then an hour at the end of the day. And as satisfying as it was to volunteer on his school's interfraternity council for several hours a week, perhaps that could wait until after he had locked down his new job. Once Todd did an honest assessment of which activities he should keep, which could be paused, and the sequencing of activities that would allow the most time and energy to devote to his job search, he dove into his job search with laser focus. It wasn't long before he got the results he'd been hoping for from day one!

You can follow Todd's lead too, and assess where you're spending your time and energy - the "big rocks" in your day and week. And I'll give you a hint, the things you're excited to spend time on and devoting the most time and energy too, are generally your current priorities! Actions speak louder than words. Take an honest look at what those things are. If your job search is not included among them, and you're not getting the results you want, then it's time to do some reevaluating and consider which activities you can put on the back burner for now. Just as there are only so many hours in a day, there is a limit to the physical and mental energy you have available every day. To avoid getting stuck in frustration, do an honest assessment of where you're investing your time and energy. See what needs to change to prioritize your job search, while realizing that this might require some tough decisions and saying "no" to things you normally enjoy (for the time being). Believe that in the end those sacrifices will be worth it - emotionally, physically, and professionally.

Be Authentic

Monique worked with investments in New York City and prided herself in knowing the economic intricacies of her industry down to the most granular details. When her investment firm downsized and Monique unexpectedly found herself out of work, she essentially shook it off as a temporary inconvenience, assuming that in the roaring economy and with her education, knowledge and background, getting reemployed would be a breeze.

Monique found her predictions of success confirmed - at first - when it seemed like nearly every resume and application she sent out, resulted in an interview. The problem was, in her words, she was "bombing" in all her interviews - without exception or explanation. She was mystified, frustrated, and for the first time in memory since the crash of '08 - fearful.

This is where the tactic of mock interviewing takes center stage! If, like Monique, you're going on interview after interview, and getting nothing but rejection in return, rather than getting stuck in frustration, find an accountability partner (a job coach, colleague, friend, or family member) and do as many mock/virtual interviews as it takes to find out what's not working. Also make sure to mix it up with phone, video and face to face scenarios. You want to have as realistic a picture of your situation as possible.

This is exactly what Monique did, and after just one mock interview, the answer became clear – she was *massively* over preparing and then in the interviews, overthinking each question. The feedback provided to Monique was that by the time she walked in and shook the interviewer's hand, she was a walking, talking human computer of investment knowledge, current market stats and an encyclopedia of industry jargon right on the tip of her tongue.

To be clear, being prepared for interviews is a positive thing. But over-preparing – overthinking all possible angles of potential questions and memorizing overly detailed, complicated answers – can backfire. It can muddy the authenticity and humanity of your personal brand impression, ultimately alienating the interviewer. Overthinking takes you out of the present moment and prevents the creation of natural rapport between yourself and the other person.

I can personally relate to this, having over-prepared for different media interviews over the years, memorizing every word of my responses to each possible question in advance. Let's just say that I was not at my "brand best" in those particular interviews! I learned my lesson and now prepare by reviewing potential questions in advance, preparing talking points to keep me on track, looking them over a few times, and then from there, trusting my instincts – and myself – and going for it. This helps me stay in the moment and connect better with the interviewer while talking.

That's exactly the "authenticity first" tactic that Monique applied, once she realized how she was shooting herself in the foot by over-preparing before and overthinking during her interviews. She pulled back, and learned to trust in her ample knowledge of her industry, took up meditation to learn how to be present in the moment, and, above all, practiced being "Monique" (versus "human encyclopedia") in one mock interview after another, until her true personality and authenticity finally shone through!

In job interviews, there are certain answers you can prepare for in advance (like tell me your about yourself or your strengths). But what you can't practice, is being yourself. That needs to come naturally, because hiring managers are not just assessing whether your resume, knowledge, and experience are a fit for the organization - they're looking at whether YOU as a human being are!

It's crucial we acknowledge "chemistry" as an essential element in hiring. Assuming most candidates in an industry will have comparable levels of knowledge, it's often the most likeable candidate that will get a job offer. Even when a knowledge deficit is revealed, a hiring manager may feel its easily taught and likeability or values alignment takes precedence. This may seem odd or unfair, but just for a moment place yourself in a manager's shoes who has very real concerns about a disruptive employee suddenly impacting the current workforce. One job of a manager is managing workforce chemistry. You should research the values and culture of the organization and see yourself as additive to that chemistry and you will come across as such.

Chemistry is so essential because candidates must fit within the culture of an organization. This is a two-way street and you should be as observant as possible assessing whether you see yourself as a cultural fit at that workplace.

Throw Yourself A Party

Feeling overwhelmed with frustration? Throw yourself a "pity party." What is your very favorite indulgence when you're feeling low? For one client stuck in frustration with her search, it was putting on a pair of ratty bunny slippers and eating a bowl of her favorite ice cream. Our coach gave her permission to throw herself a 24 hour "bunny slippers and ice cream" party where she wasn't expected to do any job search activities. At the end of those 24 hours though, she would be expected to end the party, let go of her frustration and get back to work on the job search. For others who don't own bunny slippers, this could mean simply taking an afternoon for fishing or hiking, or spending an evening at the beach or boardwalk. Pick the activity that you love doing when not job searching that doesn't cost a lot of money.

Self-Reflection

As with any emotion, it would be highly unlikely that you've never felt the way you're feeling now, ever before in your life. Therefore, grab your journal and think back to all the various times you've felt frustrated in your life - whether from not getting something you wanted (or thought you wanted), feeling unable to move out of a negative situation, or otherwise. How did you move past your frustration in those times? Did you develop any coping mechanisms or strategies for dealing with your emotions that perhaps until now you've forgotten about? You can apply this tactic to any of the "Loss" and "Paralyzing" emotions.

Develop A Realistic Plan

When you're stuck feeling frustrated, it's not the time to aim for perfection. An ideal job search plan with the bar set too high, almost guarantees failure. This is the time instead to develop a realistic plan of action - small but consistent steps you are reasonably sure you'll be able to complete, day after day. Each step will move you further along while also giving you the satisfaction of checking things off your "to do" list. Having a daily list of doable, tactical items will help you conquer frustration simply by putting yourself in a position to complete those items, one by one, with consistency being the name of the game.

Pair this tactic with an accomplishment log that you complete at the end of every day or every week, where you write down ALL your job search actions taken or your key successes. Having a realistic plan of daily action combined with an accomplishment log where you record (and acknowledge and celebrate) your results will help redirect you from the idea of "perfect," which is all but impossible to accomplish and leads to frustration, to "done."

Set A Negotiating Target

The offer negotiation can be a stressful and frustrating part of the job search too, especially when you aren't being offered what you believe you deserve, whether in salary, equity, benefits, or all of the above. Get clear early on and before interviews about the top priorities you want to negotiate for. Salary, time off, a flexible work schedule, title, responsibilities, telecommuting - what's most important for you? (Unfortunately "everything" is not really an option here and if your answer is "everything" you haven't reflected enough on your circumstances). Knowing this upfront can keep you focused on your priorities during the negotiation to move the conversation to where you want it to go. You might not get everything you want, but if you keep your goals clear, this tactic may help you get to a solution you can live with and get to work.

Do Your Homework

A common source of frustration, in job searching and in life, comes from a lack of preparation. If you do your homework and find out what you need to know in advance of a situation, you are much less likely to experience the frustration that comes from going in unprepared. Knowledge and preparation add to your Career EQ power. Don't just "show up" to job situations without putting in the advance work and expect things to magically work out in your favor. It does not work that way, in any industry or in any type of economy.

This also applies to setting realistic expectations. Expecting to make top dollar right out of college for instance, like people who have worked in the industry for years earn is not realistic. You need a track record in order to progress to that level. This is another example of where doing your homework is critical in avoiding needless frustration.

Key Points:

- Much of the frustration during a job search comes from the lack of control a job seeker has over their search. The longer the search goes, the more that frustration can grow.

- Behavior changes, feeling overwhelmed, and decision paralysis are common offshoots of frustration to be aware of.

- Key tactics in managing frustration include managing your time, energy, actions, and attention.

Chapter 8

Anxiety

Since both fear and anxiety are job search emotions covered in this book, I feel it's important to briefly make a distinction between the two. Experts state that fear is connected to "a real or perceived imminent threat," while anxiety results from a more unknown vaguely defined one.[1] In her book "*Hack Your Anxiety*," Dr. Alicia Clark states that "anxiety is an emotion characterized by feelings of tension, worried thoughts and physical changes." She goes to say that "anxiety is both something each of us might define a little differently, and yet something we know when we feel it." There can be concrete reasons behind our feelings of unease, like the memory of a specific blown job interview from your past, but often anxiety about "going out there" to look for a job is less clear in its origin.

Anxiety doesn't even have to be directly related to job loss to still feel it about your job search. At IMPACT Group, we work with many people who want to explore the idea of leaving one job to find another one that's a better fit, but the idea of making the transition triggers a general state of anxiety in them. The more they contemplate the idea of leaving the security of their current job and going out in search of the X factor of a new job, the more anxiety they may feel about the situation. This state of anxiety is not connected to a specific

---

[1] *American Psychiatric Association. Diagnostic and Statistical Manual of Mental Disorders. 5th edition. Washington DC; 2013. https://dsm. psychiatryonline.org/doi/10.1176/appi.books.9780890425596.dsm05*

fear, but rather a nervousness about what jobs are out there, what the process of transitioning will entail, and the wisdom of their decision to leave behind job security to take a risk. Once they have the right information, however, including clarity on their personal brand and the best career and company matches for it, the anxiety can begin to subside. But when it first shows up, just like the other emotions we've been exploring, anxiety can disrupt at best, and at worst, completely paralyze your job search.

Assess:
Is anxiety showing up in your job search?

1. **When your mind turns to thinking of the job search, do you start to feel uneasiness and/or agitation?**
2. **Do you have more negative thoughts about getting your next position than positive thoughts?**
3. **Do you find yourself not applying for jobs that are a good fit for you?**
4. **Do you catastrophize every rejection, believing that "the worst" has happened?**
5. **Do you find yourself constantly overthinking conversations you had with networking contacts and interviewers?**

How Anxiety Shows Up In The Job Search

Have you ever felt like no matter how hard you try and how hard you work, you still somehow come up short? That's how my team and I felt with this one particularly demanding, constantly unhappy client. No matter how hard we worked to satisfy them, it seemed like they kept raising the bar just out of our reach. The anxiety of the situation kept me up at night. There was so much on the line, but I felt helpless and that nothing could be done that we weren't already doing. I knew my anxiety wasn't changing anything but that didn't stop it. It was being constantly fed by my feelings of helplessness from watching my team diligently spin their wheels without seeing results.

In many ways this is like going for a job and coming in second to another candidate. You did everything in your power to make a great impression, you crossed all your t's and dotted all your i's - but alas, you still lost.

The best you can do in these situations is to shake it off and keep coming back. Keep stepping back into the ring and eventually you'll win a bout. That's what we did. We kept showing up for our client, day after day, doing our best. We took some bumps and bruises along the way, but we survived, were able to successfully finish the project and eventually create a strong relationship with the client. Challenges, whether on the job or while you're out looking for one, can create endless anxiety. But as long as you don't allow your anxiety to be a showstopper – you'll still be in the game. Here are some ways anxiety shows up in the job search.

Overwhelming Feelings

A generalized feeling of anxiety about the future can make it difficult or impossible to focus on the present. It might feel as if you're drowning in a sea of possibilities for action with no clear starting point. This is overwhelm, a very common feeling in the job search process with all its uncertainties, as you ask yourself - "Will I get another job?" "How long will it take?" "How will I pay the bills?" Its offshoots are avoidance, overthinking, lack of focus and scattered thinking, analysis paralysis, and doing nothing – all results of anxiety emotionally blocking you from taking action. Whether you're wildly throwing a bunch of darts at the wall hoping one will stick, or sitting in the corner grasping that first dart nervously in your fist, the net result of "no results" is the same.

Anxiety and its effects are closely connected to your body's built-in "fight, flight or freeze" response, with the adrenaline released by anxiety, causing your racing, stressed-out mind to choose between "fight" – confronting the source of your anxiety, "flight" – avoiding it, or "freeze" – paralysis. While avoidance and paralysis are self-explanatory, the "fight" in this scenario, can lead to overthinking or in some cases making inappropriate decisions in the job search (like sharing nasty things about past employers in the middle of an interview). It can also cause a candidate to cast too wide of a net in their job search, creating countless (sometimes conflicting) versions of their resume, and applying for every job under the sun whether it's a fit or not.

The other side of the "fight or flight" anxiety coin can be positive – spurring you into productive action. But if you're either unaware of or not properly dealing with your anxiety, it's more likely to show up on the negative side of the coin, sabotaging your job search efforts.

Take Control Checkpoint: Overwhelm

How do you typically deal with feeling overwhelmed - at work and in your personal life? Fight, flight or freeze? It's better to explore this ahead of time and activate self-awareness now, than when anxiety, or even panic, hits in the moment.

Self-Sabotage

Job seekers make many assumptions and hold beliefs about the job search that can eventually lead to anxiety. For example, "Sending as many resumes as humanly possible will only help me get a job," or "I should be able to get a job in a month" (which as we've learned is a challenging assumption regardless of the job market), or "I can use the same job search methods I did ten years ago and be successful," and "Having a LinkedIn profile isn't important." These types of beliefs about the job search and other unfounded assumptions can sabotage your efforts and extend the time of the job search. What conscious or unconscious assumptions and beliefs about the job search might you be carrying that could be a source of self-sabotage down the line? Take some time to sit with this thought and make a list of what comes up.

> **Brand Angle: Branding to Reduce Anxiety**
>
> **Anxiety about a job search can be a cumulative effect from years of workplace insecurities that have built up and in some cases labels that people have allowed others to attach to them. Engaging in the personal branding process is a way to unpack those insecurities and labels and bring them into the light. Identify what these insecurities are, then acknowledge and release them, replacing them with your personal brand of you at your best so you can move forward without the extra baggage.**

Social Anxiety

Social anxiety is a specific type of anxiety, commonly experienced by introverted individuals, which makes the idea of speaking to others, whether in networking or interview situations, a nerve wracking experience. This is particularly true since about half of the job search process is connected to networking. Toss in the component of constant rejection that's par for the course, and any existing social anxiety can go right through the roof, making the experience outright painful.

Social anxiety and anxiety in general can also keep an individual hiding behind their computer where they feel safe, away from real human people. Going out into a world full of unknowns and searching for a job in person can be a terrifying prospect to someone suffering from social anxiety. Confining their job search to the sterile internet without actually connecting with people (either in person or virtually) is their way of coping with that anxiety by focusing on something over which they *do* have control. Unfortunately, it makes for an incomplete and much less effective job search.

Tactics To Overcome Anxiety

Focus On What You CAN Control

David, a bright, friendly guy, worked as a pharmacologist, researching and testing drugs to study their effects. When he was laid off from the smaller drug company where he worked for over a decade, his biggest worry was an extremely specific one - what might happen in an interview. One of David's motivations for his line of work, was that since he was a toddler, he'd suffered from epileptic seizures. The seizures could strike at any time and without warning, including, in David's mind, smack dab in the middle of a job interview, blowing his job opportunity. Picturing this possibility made him extremely anxious.

But rather than using this as an excuse to avoid interviews, David took a different approach, one that he considered "only fair" to potential employers in light of the circumstances. As part of his job applications, he included a special letter describing his seizure disorder in detail, explaining that he might have a seizure during the interview and, based on this information, if a potential employer would prefer to avoid this risk by passing him over for an interview, he would completely understand.

It was very important to David to be upfront with potential employers, and he was right that giving them advance warning that this sudden and even scary scenario could happen, was fair. The issue, however, was with the *way* in which he chose to communicate it. Working with David, we agreed to adjust his strategy, so rather than warning employers at the very beginning of the recruitment process, he would submit his resume and application without any disclaimers, attract interest based on his work history and accomplishments, field and accept interview requests, and then schedule interviews. At the beginning of interviews, however, after the initial greeting and making the all-important first impression, he would then tactfully and without making a huge deal out of it, describe his medical situation to the employer. He would frame it as, "Yes, I have this condition, I am taking medication for it, and it is under control. However, there is a small chance that this event might happen and here is what you should do in that event."

By approaching it this way, rather than potentially alarming employers before they even had a review his resume, David greatly increased his odds of success in moving through the job search process. As a result, an employer who saw his talent, respected his approach, and had empathy for him hired him on the spot!

As is true in most cases of anxiety, the source of David's concern had a legitimate foundation and it was fair to let employers know about it. But by telling them *too* early in the process, he was inadvertently making it a bigger deal than it had to be, potentially allowing the emotion to sabotage his job search process. Instead, he opted to take charge of what he *could* control - the way in which he presented the information about his condition - as a way of controlling employers' perceptions about it. This decision ultimately went a long way in calming David's anxiety, making him much more appealing to employers, including the one who hired him.

While the best practices for managing reactions to a disability are not entirely black and white, David's new approach makes sure that he had the interview in hand before disclosing his situation. We've worked with other people with unique circumstances where after scheduling the interview, a woman sent an email in a relaxed tone informing the interviewer, "Just so you know and are prepared, I'm completely bald from a physical condition and don't wear a wig." This allows the interviewer to not have to struggle with the elephant in the room when they really should be listening to your great responses! As a side note, this woman also made her authentic approach to her disability a strength and core to her brand.

Are there any job search behaviors you're currently engaging in that might be harming your search or at minimum, not helping it? Are you allowing your anxiety to disguise itself as "due diligence" and throwing up disclaimers and apologies to potential employers that are really unnecessary? If you are, but you believe the details are important, consider changing the timing or delivery of the information so it's less of a potential barrier in the hiring process.

Of course not every disability or unique situation needs to be addressed during the hiring process. Pregnancy is one of those situations that some people choose to disclose and some don't. My recommendation is two-fold: focus on building great relationships during the interview process and go with what you feel is ethically right. Some people feel from an ethical point of view that they need to share that information before receiving an offer, or they feel that the relationship with their future manager might be jeopardized by not sharing their status. In that case, get the employer really interested in you first. Early in the hiring process, it is easy for an employer to not move you forward and give some other reason when it was the pregnancy that actually scared them away. But once they know how amazing you are and see that you are a perfect fit with the organization, if you are the person they really want, chances are they will move forward regardless. However, since a woman's pregnancy does not have to be disclosed, there's nothing wrong with not saying anything.

Practice Networking

Julie was struggling with what for her, was the most challenging part of the job search - networking. A quiet and reserved person by nature, what specifically ratcheted up the anxiety were awkward pauses in conversations. She even half-joked about how she was afraid she might "run out of the room" if a moment of silence became too unbearable.

Julie feared her more withdrawn nature and social anxiety around conversations, especially ones prone to pauses and lulls, like in networking and interviews, would make her come across as unsure of herself and her abilities. The anxiety she felt around the "talking" parts of the job search carried through to her resume and job applications too, where she downplayed her strengths and career history. Julie was allowing her anxiety around awkward conversations to dominate all her job search actions.

The tactic used to help Julie, was finding the right person to add to her Super Team to have "practice conversations" with. In her case, this was a real life employer and therefore someone used to interviewing people. Most importantly, she found someone *super* extroverted and talkative, essentially eliminating any chances of those awkward pauses that made Julie so anxious. Meeting with her conversation practice partner, doing mock interviews, and simply engaging in casual conversations, increased Julie's confidence.

After enough of these practice conversations, the idea that a pause in a conversation might make her flee the scene, seemed highly unlikely to Julie. As a final insurance policy, she made a list of conversation topics, questions, and talking points that she could memorize and use, should conversation lulls pop up during her networking and interviewing situations. For this introvert, rather than giving in and allowing anxiety to dull her shine, she put in the work, invested in preparation, and it paid off when, within a couple months she landed her next job!

If the idea of networking creates this same type of anxiety in you, see how you can follow in Julie's footsteps and find a partner to practice networking with. The more you do it and the more people you do it with, the less anxiety provoking of an experience that it will be for you. If you're anxious about public speaking in general, consider seeking out your local Toastmasters chapter. You'll meet new people, practice speaking in public and even practice getting comfortable with pauses and silence - a valuable technique in networking and interviewing.

Change Your Language

Claire was an attorney who had been with the same firm since graduating law school twenty-five years ago. When her firm was acquired by a larger one and she was laid off, Claire almost instantly spun out into what felt like an all-out anxiety storm - and with good reason. She was the sole breadwinner for her stay-at-home husband and three children. On top of that, this was the first and only job she'd ever had, and it was basically handed to her through a direct referral by her law school dean. Claire had never really had to look for a job and had no idea what the job search process entailed. This anxiety about the unknown combined with the financial pressure of supporting her family felt paralyzing to the otherwise confident, Ivy League attorney who could level opposing counsel in the courtroom, but hadn't a clue as to how to write a resume.

First Claire got to work diligently learning everything she could about all the tactics of a successful job search, step by step. But even then, she found herself experiencing anxiety that was keeping her from moving forward.

Peeling the layers away of Claire's uncertainty about the job search process, we discovered something interesting but not that surprising at the core, especially as a person who focuses on language for a living. A big part of her anxiety was in the *language* of looking for a job. One word in particular that set off her nerves, was "networking." As an attorney, she had been to networking dinners and mixers where the focus was more on new developments in the legal field, a conversation where Claire felt comfortable. Where she did *not* feel comfortable, was in thinking about networking in a job search context, where she imagined positioning conversations to shine a giant spotlight on herself. The idea of calling her colleagues and "pitching" herself to get a job - which is how Claire thought of "networking" in the job search context, made her extremely anxious.

The simple tactic Claire needed to move out of anxiety and into action was a change in job search language, specifically the word "networking." So, "networking" became "reconnecting" - as in, simply reaching out to an old friend and having a casual, social conversation. Gone was the idea of what she thought networking had to be: summoning the courage to cold call a fellow attorney and "sell herself."

Once Claire was able to make that language swap and change her negative associations and therefore emotions around networking, her anxiety subsided and she was able to move forward in her job search. One of her "social calls" was to a former coworker who was now with a different large firm. Her coworker, with whom she shared a mutual respect, was glad to reconnect with Claire, and when a new position with his firm opened up, he happily referred her and Clare got the job!

> ### *Take Control Checkpoint*: Job Search Language
>
> Review the language of the job search, preferably out loud - laid off, out of work, looking for a job, networking, interviewing, salary negotiation, etc. Are there any words or phrases that make you feel anxious? How could you rephrase them in a way that feels better to you?

Stop The Chain Reaction

You know them - the negative, anxiety-producing, and at times outright malicious thoughts that get stuck in your head while you're awake and wake you up when you're trying to sleep. For me, waking up in the middle of the night spinning these worst case scenarios around in my head, is one of the worst kinds of anxiety. These thoughts effectively take over my brain at night, but sometimes the next morning, by the light of day, when I reexamine the same thoughts you wonder what on earth you were freaking out about.

The key here is to cut down the chain reaction before it has time to ignite. Whether anxiety producing "what if" thoughts are keeping you up at night or disrupting your day, see how you can reframe your anxious thoughts, especially the more "catastrophic" ones. Yes, bad things can happen - in life and in your job search. But how can you prevent that one thought from consuming and controlling your brain? Find the ringleader.

When you find yourself in this chain reaction of anxious thoughts, rather than trying to suppress the thoughts (pleading with your brain to "shut up!"), consider writing them all down without censoring yourself. For each one ask, "So what?" What is the root of this feeling? What's the worst thing that could happen if this came true? How can I keep this from happening? Many times, simply shining a spotlight on the anxious thought will be enough to dissolve it. Eliminate the chain reaction by sucking the power out of all its pieces. As author Susan Packard says in her book "*Fully Human: 3 Steps to Grow Your Emotional Fitness in Work, Leadership, and Life*" - "name it, claim it, let it go."

Get Clarity

For some people, the idea of a "job search" is a fuzzy, out-of-focus picture. Lack of clarity on what it actually takes to get a job, especially when compounded with the stress of a recent job loss, can set off anxiety and if there's a potential career change involved, create a sense of overwhelm.

If this is you, make a list of every single question you have about the job search, all the unknowns – from the largest questions ("how long will it take?") to the smallest ("how do I update my LinkedIn profile headline?"). There are no stupid questions and no details too small to address, especially if they will move you out of anxiety and into action. With greater access to information, answers, and resources than ever before, you'll be able to begin to answer each of these questions – either through your own research or by seeking out help from others. There is absolutely no reason to sit alone in the darkness, suffering from the anxiety of not knowing.

If you have anxiety because you're not clear on your personal brand - who you are, what you offer, and what you want to do - take the time to get answers to these questions as well. Brand clarity means you're taking more intentional, specific action steps in your job search. This clarity will help build your confidence and also improve how people view you because you'll be seen as articulate, competent, and self-assured!

Move One Rock

Stare at a mountain of rocks for too long and it will absolutely seem unmovable. Similarly, it might sound like a big task to move from anxiety-induced overwhelm into action, but in reality, it takes only one, initial, often small task to get the ball rolling. Rather than seeing the job search in front of you like a mountain of rocks needing to be moved, focus on moving one single rock in front of you, such as:

- Sign up for an online course to sharpen one of your career skills.
- Do research about current market salaries in your industry.
- Set a date for completing your resume, rewriting your cover letter, or writing your elevator speech.
- Refresh (or set up) your LinkedIn profile.

Make a list of every single rock that needs to be moved and add deadlines to each one. That will become your job search action plan.

This tactic also falls under the category of focusing on things you *do* have control over, which is a huge deal in a typical job search full of unknowns. Taking structured, incremental steps can move you out of anxiety created overwhelm and paralysis, all the way into actual excitement about the job search!

Unplug

There was a time not long ago, when job searches were limited to the telephone, mail, fax machine, and then personal computer. Whenever you stepped away from any of these forms of communication, you got a break from the stress and anxiety of the job search. With 24/7 access to smart technology this is no longer the case. Our phones, tablets, laptops, and tech wearables have become so ingrained in our daily lives that sometimes we might not even realize how often we're "checking" them for updates, including responses from employers. Thanks to your smartphone, you can literally get rejected for a job while sitting down to an otherwise pleasant family dinner. With smart technology, breaks from job searching no longer exist unless you make the *conscious* choice to create them.

If you find, especially after reading this chapter, that you are prone to anxiety, I highly recommend creating breaks and "rules" around smart technology. One example of a rule might be to set up a separate email that you use only for your job search. This will be valuable, for instance, if you're checking your regular personal email for a delivery update on that Amazon order you've been waiting for, but with job hunting emails mixed in, you accidentally fall down the rabbit hole of replying to job-related emails for hours on end. Creating a separate email for your job search will help you separate it from the rest of your life - physically and emotionally.

Also consider setting your phone aside - or at least turning the notifications off - for a set number of hours each day to give your mind the opportunity to consciously disconnect from your job search. This allows you to reserve all that emotional capital that you'll need for the duration of the job search (which is a marathon, not a sprint). Career EQ means understanding how your emotions work and setting boundaries accordingly for yourself, especially when you find yourself under the influence of potentially detrimental outside factors like technology.

Take Control Checkpoint: Online Habits

Look at your current online habits. Which ones need to be adjusted and/or streamlined to reduce "reaction anxiety" and ultimately creating a more pleasant job search for you?

Volunteer

One Career EQ raising tactic for anxiety and really any of the emotions we've been talking about, is to volunteer, even for an hour or two a week. Loss and paralyzing emotions have a way of festering the more you sit and dwell on them. By finding a way to get "outside yourself" and focus on helping others, you're moving your attention away from those emotions and toward making a positive impact on others. Find a way to be of service to others and treat it like any of your other job search tactics.

Key Points:

- **Anxiety can come from not having all the details or having the incorrect ones. Get the facts!**

- **Be aware ahead of time what triggers anxiety for you and your best ways for dealing with it to avoid any anxiety "chain reactions."**

- **When feeling overwhelmed by anxiety, determine which factors in your job search you *can* control and what baby steps you can take in your action plan to keep moving forward.**

- **Create time where you are free from passive notifications of emails, texts or calls that will cause you to relinquish control over personal time. Declare certain periods (like dinner time with family) free zones where you will not check messages on any platform related to your job search.**

Chapter 9

Loneliness

Loneliness doesn't always mean a person directly acknowledging, "I'm lonely." It's more likely to show up in often subtle day-to-day behaviors. A recently unemployed person stops returning their friends' phone calls and texts. A few weeks in, they cancel their gym membership and their once active social media accounts, grow dark. Within a couple months, friends and family members are concerned about their once sociable loved one who now seems to spend every waking moment at home behind a computer, doing little else other than looking for a job, eating, and sleeping.

The speed that loneliness sets in can vary. Sometimes it can be immediate, with withdrawal setting in when an individual, particularly one who worked in a more social workspace like an office, goes from experiencing dozens of different interactions every day – to none outside of family. Or, for others, loneliness is a slow insidious process embedding itself over a longer period of time.

One of the reasons that loneliness is the emotion closing out the sections covering loss and paralyzing emotions, is that loneliness can be the cumulative effect of those feelings. As the job search goes on, especially in long searches, daily struggles with grief, anger, fear, denial, and anxiety, can come together in a perfect storm of isolation, where the job seeker essentially "checks out" - no longer mentally or physically able to engage with the world anymore. But, just like with all the previous emotions covered, there *are* specific tactics that can be used to move through loneliness, re-engage with the world (especially with those who desire to help you!), and move forward through the storm, to the light at the end of the tunnel.

The symptoms of loneliness are very similar, sometimes overlapping, with depression. It's crucial you pay close attention and seek advice to avoid a flare up of clinical depression.

Assess:
Is loneliness showing up in your job search?

1. **Are you less likely to engage in activities that interested you before?**
2. **Are you watching a lot more TV (including streaming, binge watching) than usual?**
3. **Are you spending significantly more time on social media than usual (outside of specific job search/ personal brand reasons)?**
4. **Are you missing meals or eating more than you normally do? Have your eating habits changed in other ways (eating less healthy for instance, eating while working on your computer, etc.)?**
5. **Has it been much longer than usual since you've left the house and/or spent time with friends and family? Don't go by memory - actually look at your calendar to see?**

How Loneliness Shows Up In The Job Search

The Net As A Safety Net

The internet is an efficient job search tool, replacing many hours of mailing resumes, searching through want ads in multiple newspapers, making individual phone calls to companies and then pounding the pavement to apply in person at each one - activities that job seekers of the past endured. On the other hand, when used in excess or as the *exclusive* job search tool, the internet can become more of an interpersonal safety net. Hiding out online offers a convenient excuse to avoid in-person networking and other potentially nerve wracking human interactions. Relying solely (or mostly) on the internet for your job search can make the already lonely process of looking for a job even more isolating.

An over-reliance on the internet doesn't provide tremendously helpful feedback either. There's a difference between the human feedback you get from your Super Team, a coach in a mock interview, and the social cues received in networking conversations, versus an email folder full of "sent" applications and automated rejections. None of the latter tell you a thing about what you're doing right and where you need improvement. The internet has its value, but only when used in conjunction with actual in-person job search tactics.

Take Control Checkpoint: Online Time

How much time are you spending online every day in regards to your job search? Designate one day (or several days) and keep a log to track your online time and note in your journal how you feel at the end of your internet time. If you're not happy with the results of this audit, designate specific times of day as "online time" and stick to that schedule. After a week of following this process, return to your journal and note any differences in how you felt when logging off.

Social Isolation

Isolation, whether intentional or unintentional, can show up as a sign of loneliness and also a direct result of it. Many job seekers, shortly after losing their jobs, will start phasing out what were once enjoyable social activities, isolating themselves from friends, often in an effort to conserve financial resources. In extreme cases, they'll stop leaving the house at all except for essential purposes, relying solely on technology to find a job.

Social isolation can be caused by feelings of embarrassment over being unemployed, a fear of spending money in light of a loss of income, or sometimes the feeling that "I don't deserve to have any fun until I'm earning an income again." Some might feel that being "social" sends a message to the world that they're not taking their job search seriously. This is especially true of breadwinners and even more so with male job seekers.

One man decided at the last minute not to attend his 25th high school reunion, something he'd previously been looking forward to attending. He'd been to all his previous reunions and had kept up a set of close friendships over the years. Prior to losing his job he'd even bought a new suit for the occasion. But then came the unexpected layoff and, feeling ashamed, embarrassed to admit he was without a job, he made up a "family emergency" and bowed out of the event. In his mind, he would probably be the only person in the room looking for a job so, even in a packed room surrounded by friends, he might as well be alone on a desert island.

For this man and so many other job seekers, it was easier to socially isolate himself than to confront, let alone talk about or worse, answer questions from others, about being "unemployed." Social isolation can feel like the safest option, even a survival strategy, especially when going out and being around other people can mean fielding questions about their job search, questions that they may not be ready to answer. "How's your job search going?" from the most well-meaning friend, can feel like a soul piercing dagger to an individual experiencing the isolation, shame and the myriad other emotions wrapped up inside of it like anxiety, frustration, and fear.

More Work Options, Less Isolation

For workers who spend more time in person with their coworkers, in some cases more than with their own families, work life and social life become interchangeable. In these cases, unemployment can be a jarring shift. You go from being effectively surrounded by people at work for forty plus hours a week, to being home alone scrolling through job listings.

One potential positive we're seeing with today's more flexible work environments, is a decrease in the social isolation and loneliness that used to come almost automatically with a job loss. As options like telecommuting become more and more common, workers rely less on the workplace as the chief source of their social interactions. They're more likely to have a life outside of work.

Some might call this "better work life balance" but in actuality today's workers might not be consciously "balancing" anything. Younger workers could simply be staying connected to friends the way they have since childhood – virtually, as opposed to prior decades where the workplace was a significant social pillar. Workers today are also less likely to stay with the same company for many years, let alone decades, making it less likely that their "work friends" are their only ones.

Tactics To Overcome Loneliness

Seek Positive Feedback

One of the greatest sources of loneliness in the job search can be the "resume black hole." Candidates often spend hours every day, sending resume after resume and job application after job application into what seems like a bottomless virtual pit of faceless companies. After a few straight months of this, Tim was frustrated and ready to call it quits on the whole operation. The day-to-day cycle of clicking send and then either hearing nothing back at all or getting automated responses or rejections from employers, was depressing and isolating to him. Staring forlornly into his computer screen day after day, only made emotional matters worse. Tim was immersed in a sea of negative feedback which triggered emotions such as anxiety and sadness, and as a result, he completely isolated himself from others, including his wife. As a way of avoiding potentially uncomfortable "how's the job search going honey?" conversations with her, he would spend almost every waking moment in his home office, parked at his desk behind the computer. Most times, he would even have his meals there, clicking away, sending email after email into the black hole, getting back zero beneficial feedback that might help his search.

What Tim needed to shift his emotions and his perspective on his job search, was positive feedback. He needed to be reminded of ALL the great things he had accomplished in his career so far, all his achievements, and everything he brought to the table. He eventually found this in an accountability partner through a local job search support group. Spending time with someone who could objectively point out these things lifted Tim's spirits immensely. So much so that he was finally willing to get out from behind the computer, sit down and have dinner with his wife, and share with her what he had been feeling. In doing so, he realized how spending more time with his wife would help him to open up and vent his emotions in a healthy way rather than keeping them bottled up and then dealing with the repercussions of doing so.

Tim's decision to open up about what he was going through, unleashed a flood of positive feedback from his wife who had been worried sick about him and desperately wanted to help. Hearing that something as simple as positive validation could be helpful in cutting through the silence and negative feedback of the "resume black hole" was music to her ears. It wasn't long before Tim felt up to getting out of his office and attending networking events where he gained valuable leads, including the one that would lead him to his next position.

This has fast become one of our Career EQ themes – technology has immense benefits in the job search, but if you over rely on it, and worse, use it as an excuse to isolate yourself from other people, including potential in-person job search leads, there can be negative practical and emotional consequences. The point and click monotony of electronically submitting your resume over and over again, and getting either nothing or negative feedback in return, can lead to feelings of frustration, sadness and, with only your computer screen to interact with, loneliness.

One way to snap out of this negative spiral is by actively and intentionally seeking positive feedback from others about your value, skills, work experience, and other positive aspects of your brand impression. This is not some artificial ego boost. If seeking objective validation of your value allows you to keep moving forward in your search - then it's a productive, useful job search tool like any other. Your Super Team is a perfect place to start.

Sample questions could include:
-What do you perceive my strengths to be?
-Why would you hire me?
-What do you value about me as a person?

Make New Friends

Kelli, a software engineer at a technology start-up in Boston, placed great value in the friendships she'd formed on the job over the last two years. Working sometimes 60 hours a week, her career was pretty much her life, with no time to devote to outside friendships or extracurricular activities. Tightly bonded with her colleagues as they all worked enthusiastically to make the startup a success, Kelli had lunch every day with a different coworker, or sometimes a vendor or other business contact connected to the company. She and her work friends would also frequently get together for drinks on Fridays and occasionally even mani-pedis on a Saturday (usually with mimosas!).

So it was a double slap in the face when Kelli was first laid off by the suddenly struggling start-up after a failed round of VC funding, and was then abandoned by the people she'd considered friends - good friends. After initially checking in on her, the friends Kelli felt so close to stopped reaching out, and then took longer and longer to reply to her outreaches. She was no longer invited to the happy hours or Saturday outings. Kelli was stunned and a little heartbroken at the sudden loss of what she once considered to be close friendships. It might have been a case of "out of sight, out of mind" for her busy colleagues, but that didn't make the loneliness sting less. The reality was that her "work friends" were just that, and from their point of view, those friendships expired the day she was fired.

Within a short period of time Kelli found herself feeling totally isolated with an almost overwhelming sense of loneliness. Add in the feeling of betrayal by people whom she'd trusted, and she was not keen at all on the idea of going out and making new friends, even if it meant relieving her feelings of loneliness.

Rather than telling her to "go make friends," her coach reframed it as "networking," a crucial part of the process of landing a new job. Ambitious and career driven by nature, Kelli agreed to this tactic, also seeing the positive that another job, another workplace, would give her the chance to start over and forge newer (and hopefully stronger) friendships.

She started by seeking out her local professional organizations with like-minded people in her industry, attending various networking mixers and meals where she inevitably picked up job leads and made new connections. She liked one group well enough that she began volunteering to help out at their events where she made even more contacts. Then, not wanting to fall into the same trap of having one source of friends again, she eventually started to look at building relationships outside of professional networks.

One of her favorite activities that she had abandoned in recent years was tennis, and for Kelli, this quickly became a social activity she invested more time in. So she found her way to a weekend tennis league. Soon, Kelli found a new job and new co-workers, but this time, with one foot firmly entrenched in her tennis tribe, her "work friends" were far from her only ones. As she became more involved in outside activities, she began to recognize the benefits of establishing a work/social life balance in her friendships.

Relying on work as your sole source of a social life can lead to sudden social isolation and loneliness if and when you lose your job. As convenient as it is to depend on the people you work with for any semblance of a social life, it's much more beneficial to you in the long term to create friendships outside of work as well (and this also means offline!). Follow Kelli's lead and look up professional or trade organizations in your area, hobbies or leisure activities that seem appealing, meet-ups, or college courses to bolster your skill set or, just for fun, like ceramics or music appreciation. If you're currently employed, consider a strong social network an emotional buffer in the event that you need the social support down the line. If you're currently between jobs, use this extra time to branch out, explore some new activities, build your network, and hopefully make new friends in the process!

Take Control Checkpoint: Social Life

How's your social calendar looking lately? Start bringing it back to life by looking up some local professional or trade groups that hold social events and adding one to your calendar now. Even if money is tight, there are lots of free options to explore that can still fill this need.

Job Search Support Groups

If being unemployed feels like being alone on a desert island, a job search support group is the arrival of a cruise ship filled with new contacts who can relate to what you're feeling and going through. Preferably, and in the name of combating loneliness with human connection, you can find a local in-person group. But if you can't find one, finding an online group can also be a good option. If you're feeling isolated in the job search process, and reaching out to friends and family members isn't something you're ready to do, a support group of your fellow job seekers can create a safe "home base." You can share your frustrations, your feelings, and in many cases, networking contacts, tips, and resources with your fellow seekers. Being around other people in the job search will help normalize the situation, help take away any shame or guilt, and give your emotions some space and a chance to breathe before they build up and become potential obstacles. Be careful, however, not to let these turn into gripe sessions. Keep it productive, forward focused, and centered on solutions!

Take Breaks

When you're out of work, it can be tempting to see your temporary joblessness as an urgent, time sensitive problem to be solved (which of course it often is!). But this perceived urgency can make a job seeker - especially ambitious or Type A individuals - believe that the only acceptable activity is to look for a job - constantly, during all their waking hours, and without allowing themselves leeway to do anything else. This "all in" mentality can add even more anxiety and stress to the job search and, if exercised over an extended period of time, may even lead to burnout. To keep your emotions in check and stay at the top of your mental game, take breaks. Better yet, schedule your breaks as if you're still working and each break is an important meeting that you absolutely must attend.

As a starting point, think about how you would spend your breaks at work. Maybe you'd use the time to go for a walk with a friend, run errands, or eat at a favorite restaurant. Thinking of your job search as your current job, schedule some of those same activities into your week now and then keep those appointments. Taking regular breaks gives your mind a chance to rest, ultimately making you more productive and focused. Consider also taking longer breaks maybe a couple times a month, and doing volunteer work as a way of taking the focus off yourself and helping others. No matter what kind of breaks you take, the more you go out, the more you'll be around other people, which, even in small doses, will take the edge off feelings of loneliness and support networking goals too!

> ### *Take Control Checkpoint*: Mental Health Breaks
>
> **Get your schedule out now and schedule a daily 15-30 minute "mental health" break doing an activity that you enjoy.**

Accountability Partner

As Tim learned in the earlier story, when he finally opened up to his wife about his feelings of isolation that had been building during his job search, another tactic for fending off loneliness and at the same time contributing to your job search, is to seek out an accountability partner. This person might also be searching for a job or, it could be a trusted friend. You can use your accountability partner as an excuse to take those all-important breaks, get out of the house, and also for more job search specific tactics like mock interviewing, resume reviews, and someone to objectively assess your personal brand and the impression you're making on employers, and make suggestions for improvement.

Key Points:

- One significant cause of loneliness in the job search, is limiting your efforts to the internet, and avoiding in-person (or virtual person to person) activities. Remember to regularly sign off and get seen in person!

- Having an "accountability partner" is a great way to avoid slipping into a well of isolation - start by visiting local job search/career support groups or networking organizations to see who might be looking for the same.

- Take breaks from your job search to keep feelings of isolation at bay. Schedule regular exercise, walks with friends, volunteering - anything to separate you from being in constant search mode.

- While friendships at work are very real, many dissipate or evaporate entirely when we change jobs, therefore make a conscious and deliberate effort to seek friends in a variety of places.

Part IV

Momentum!

"Inaction breeds doubt and fear. Action breeds confidence and courage. If you want to conquer fear, do not sit home and think about it. Go out and get busy."
-Dale Carnegie

Chapter 10

Self-Compassion

An extended job search can test even the most resilient person, a person who might never anticipate the toll exacted on them by their emotions. The person who begins their job search with enthusiasm and positivity and a solid support system and well-thought out strategies, after encountering a string of rejections and challenges, can find themselves in a negative spiral. As you've learned, the day-to-day and then compounded effects of emotions are real. When left unprocessed, can be devastating.

Now – It's time to rebuild. The final three Career EQ emotions are the light at the end of the tunnel!

Self-Compassion

Searching for a job can be a brutal process. A 2018 study[2] revealed that self-compassion (simply defined as being kind to yourself in the face of challenges or failure) can act as a buffer between you and the emotions that threaten to overwhelm you and derail your search. The study authors wrote: "Self-compassion can thus be viewed as a positive adaptive mindset that job seekers can apply to counteract the detrimental emotional effects of experiencing difficulties and lack of progress during job search." In other words - being unnecessarily hard

---

[2] *"Dealing with negative job search experiences: The beneficial role of self-compassion for job seekers' affective responses."* Journal of Vocational Behavior 106 (2018) pgs 165-179. Kreemers, van Hooft and van Vianen.

on yourself only makes every step that much harder to get through.

That's the situation that Sylvia, a longtime Human Resources Benefits Administrator, found herself in. A long, emotionally grueling job search had left her confidence and willpower shaken. Things only got worse when she was named a top finalist for a position at a company she was really excited about. She aced the job interview but was then thrown a last minute curveball in the form of a routine software aptitude test. Sylvia panicked. She hadn't used the particular piece of software, one that was unfortunately key to the job, in years. Sure enough, she failed the test and the job ultimately went to another candidate. The experience left her feeling humiliated at what she saw as a failure.

Sylvia's husband of 30 years was well aware of his wife's emotional state and worried about how hard she was being on herself. Fortunately, in this case, he was able to help his wife zoom out and see the big picture, refocus on her positive attributes, and remember her innate value. He reminded her of past professional successes, achievements and what life was like when she was thriving. Once she focused on that bigger picture, she was able to forgive herself, show herself some self-compassion, regroup and continue her job search.

This is a great example of the value of your Super Team in helping you show self-compassion. This can be as simple as asking yourself gently but firmly: "What purpose is it serving to beat myself up?" Because when you get stuck and ruminate in negativity, especially about a perceived "failure" like Sylvia did, it sets off a ripple effect that touches all areas of your job search - from how productive your daily activities are, to how you present yourself on your resume, to the first impression you make at interviews. Self-compassion is reminding yourself that everyone stumbles, it's okay, it does not take away from your overall value to your next employer, and more importantly, your value as a human being.

How Self-Compassion Shows Up In The Job Search

Separates Temporary From Permanent

Dr. Kristin Neff, Ph.D., author, and Associate Professor at the University of California at Berkeley, defines self-compassion as "being kind and understanding when confronted with personal failings." When emotions overwhelm you, self-compassion is your reset button. It offers an opportunity to reevaluate and reconnect with your self-worth by asking questions like - "What do you really believe to be true about yourself?" and "Does this one temporary scenario really define you as a person?" Answering such questions through a lens of forgiveness, leniency and compassion, will help you separate situational setbacks (like failing a computer aptitude test) from core beliefs about your identity. Being able to separate temporary situations from permanent beliefs helps you keep a firm grasp on your identity and the personal brand that represents it. Self-compassion reminds you that bad things might happen, but in the big picture you'll be okay.

Inspires Self-Care

When you give yourself the gift of self-compassion, you're also giving yourself permission to engage in self-care. Constantly pushing yourself, day in and day out, leaves no time for self-care, which has both physical and mental consequences. When you don't take care of yourself, you're not only compromising your health, but you're also compromising how you're projecting yourself to potential employers.

It's the little things that make a big difference. That daily walk after lunch might seem like it's sucking time away from your job search, but in reality, it might be the emotional and mental reboot you need to see your resume through fresh eyes, have more productive networking conversations, and be the best version of yourself possible in your next job interview. Allow yourself to feel self-compassion, and self-care should naturally flow. However, some find it more difficult than others.

In a 2017 Forbes.com article, writer Tami Forman said, "Self-care is not an indulgence. Self-care is a discipline. It requires tough mindedness, a deep and personal understanding of your priorities."

Take Control Checkpoint: **One Small Thing Daily**

What is ONE self-care activity, no matter how small, that you can incorporate into your schedule every single day, no matter what else is happening in your life?

Offsets Negative Thinking

Self-compassion demonstrated by thinking kindly of yourself can offset negative thinking and combat self-criticism. This is especially true in light of the "resume black hole" and other times when feedback is either nonexistent, or negative. In an informational and emotional vacuum, it's very easy for your paranoid mind to spiral into a cyclone of anxieties, fears about your perceived lack of self-worth, and other emotional mirages, where feeling is believing. Intentionally pausing to show yourself kindness, understanding and, if the need presents itself, self-forgiveness, replaces a cyclone of negativity with grace.

Tactics For Implementing Self-Compassion

Super Team & Self-Care

Jan was by nature an extremely resilient, positive person with a strong sense of self. Part of her resiliency had come from growing up as a military brat and moving constantly around the world, having to reorient herself in strange surroundings and make new friends over and over. So, when the fashion accessory company she'd worked at since college downsized and she was laid off, Jan thought - "Eh, no big deal, I've got this!" She dove headfirst into her job search with the same positive energy she attacked everything in life and in her career. Living in Los Angeles and to boot, a good economy, she had no doubt that she'd land in her next position quickly.

Jan soon learned the downside of living in a bustling metropolis in a good economy in a competitive industry - business was booming and so was competition for every available job in her field. But, true to her core personality, Jan plugged on, diligently executing on all the right tactics in her job search and with great attention to detail. Resume updated - check. Consistent online and in-person networking - check. Mock interviews with her Super Team to perfect her brand impression - check. Constantly researching developments and learning new skills in her field - check. Tapping into her natural sense of self-reliance - double check.

But as the days dragged on, even super resilient Jan eventually struggled to stay positive. The brunt of emotions she'd been fighting (and with a brave face so as not to worry her friends and family) like anxiety and fear for her financial situation took their toll. Soon, she began to spiral into limiting self-talk: "What's wrong with me? Why is everyone else finding work except me? Maybe I don't belong in fashion. Maybe I should quit and do something else!" What Jan needed in order to move forward effectively and without jeopardizing the impression she was making in her job search, was a heaping dose of self-compassion.

Jan tested the limits of her Type A personality by introducing the idea of self-care into her life. She did this as a way of showing herself kindness consistently, no matter what was happening in her job search. She leaned on her mom and older sister. She also joined a small group at her church. This served as a sounding board for her emotions, companionship, and as a reminder that her current temporary job situation did not define her as a person and complete spiritual being. (Of course this group only added to her personal and professional network as well!) Another addition was integrating a daily yoga practice into her routine that helped keep her focused. Many things may work for you whether it's meeting up with friends, making time for your favorite activity such as hiking or treating yourself to your favorite show's best season.

The sum total of Jan's efforts were a success. Showing herself kindness and forgiveness rather than allowing herself to sink into frustration and fear, shifted her entire perspective and energy toward her search and soon - her results too. Feeling like her old optimistic self again, Jan took a leap of faith and contacted a college acquaintance, whom she noticed on LinkedIn had a connection at her dream company. That connection, in turn, connected her to the company's hiring manager. She nailed all her interviews, presenting an extremely strong brand impression, edging out the competition and landing the job! As part of her email to her coach sharing the good news, Jan attached a photo of herself striking her favorite yoga pose atop nearby Big Bear Mountain where she had gone to celebrate herself and her accomplishment.

Exercise self-compassion by leaning on the people who know you best and want you to be happy, healthy, and successful - your Super Team! Also, try out various self-care activities and find one that you enjoy and can do regularly. Looking at things like proximity, cost, and time investment will ensure you're positioning yourself for self-care success!

Self-Respect

Jackie's work situation was far from perfect. In addition to consistently working long hours and feeling unappreciated for her efforts, she worked at a large organization that did not match her values. In Jackie's case, this meant a handful of male supervisors with misogynistic tendencies that were occasionally exercised toward their female subordinates - including her. Finally, after five years, Jackie had enough, and after one such incident, where she was berated by a male supervisor in front of one of her most important clients, she quit. Enough was enough!

In Jackie's mind, her upcoming job search would be emotionally brutal. It took everything she had just to get an interview, let alone land a job offer. On one hand she felt pride for standing up for herself, but on the other, she felt terror that because of her choice she might be permanently unemployable. As time dragged on, Jackie became desperate, applying to every available job she could find that she was remotely qualified for. Trapped in an emotional vice grip of her worst fears, she found herself pleading to the universe and anyone else who might be listening – "Just offer me a job, ANY job, I don't care, I don't want to be homeless!"

One morning, Jackie woke up to an offer in her inbox – a whopping offer with ridiculous pay, full benefits, and all the trimmings! But rather than celebrating, looking at the offer Jackie felt sick to her stomach. It was from her prior employer trying to woo her back. She felt tears come to her eyes as she looked at the stack of unpaid bills on the corner of her desk while also remembering how furious she felt that day in the conference room, being berated by her former supervisor in front of her favorite client. She also recalled how physically and emotionally spent she was by the end of each marathon work week. Jackie was at an almost overwhelming crossroads. Yes, this was "any job" but the idea of going back there was sickening.

Digging deep into the same supply of inner strength that freed her from the company in the first place, Jackie stepped away from her computer (and the stack of bills that seemed to be following her), grabbed her journal, got in her car and drove to the peace and quiet of a local park where she could pause, get her thoughts out on the page and hopefully make the right decision.

To her immense credit – Jackie turned down the job at her old company, and in doing so, demonstrated an intense level of self-respect and therefore self-compassion that effectively lit a fire under her job search. Jackie was determined to rise above her circumstances. She called the temp agency she'd been in occasional contact with and insisted on scheduling a check-in meeting with her contact immediately. Wearing the best possible version of herself to that meeting, Jackie essentially hit the reboot button on her entire job search. It wasn't long before she got a temporary position to make ends meet and take the financial pressure off while she continued the search for her dream job. Jackie later told us that stepping off the ledge and quitting the security of her job was the scariest but best decision of her life. Self-compassion in this case, took the form of bravery and self-respect!

Realize that the definition of self-compassion goes well beyond "self-care." Dr. Kristin Neff has described it as a combination of "mindfulness, common humanity, and self-kindness." It is whatever you personally need to do to stop, be present, acknowledge that you are a valuable, living creature deserving and in need of kindness, and then deliver on that acknowledgment.

Watch Your Language

Pay attention to the words you use to describe yourself, your beliefs, and your job search as a whole. Not just the words you write in your journal but also tune your awareness into how you talk about yourself to other people. Are you beating yourself up? Downplaying your value? Being verbally pessimistic about your odds of getting the job you want? There's a part of your subconscious mind that is processing and recording every single word and then turning those words into beliefs which then translate into actions. Ask yourself this - if your subconscious mind was a small child, would you still say the same hurtful things that maybe you've been saying about yourself? On top of that, would you then bring that child with you to your next job interview as part of your first impression? Remember, our subconscious mind goes everywhere with us and is whispering to us all the time, so make sure that it is helping to build you up!

Watching your language also means not minimizing or making light of your situation. Being out of work can be hard, and there's no reason to downplay or deny how you're feeling. Exercising compassion means being present with yourself in the moment, no matter what that moment may be. Simply telling yourself "I shouldn't be so upset about this" or "This is no big deal" or "Get over it!" won't work. Attempting to minimize your pain will not make those feelings go away. Instead, show yourself compassion and understanding for the pain you're feeling, just like you would do for a friend in pain. Give yourself the gift of acknowledgment and then healing.

Take Control Checkpoint: Negative Self-Talk

Review the journal you've been keeping during your job search and highlight any negative or self-deprecating language. Now, using the guidelines above, rewrite that language through the lens of self-compassion.

Reconnect With Your Personal Brand

Still finding yourself struggling to exercise self-compassion? This is a perfect time to reconnect with your personal brand - who you are at your professional best, outside the context of your prior company and job description? Take out your brand statement and read it a couple times and make sure you are referencing it regularly. This will remind you that while you might be between jobs, you still have the same gifts to offer others that you've always had. Reconnecting with your personal brand can spark a boost of self-confidence, it can shore up the (perhaps battered) walls of your identity, and overall, it can remind you why you're awesome. And who can't use that kind of reminder once in a while?

Identify True vs. False Beliefs

Showing yourself kindness starts with uncovering where you are being unkind to yourself. Be willing to investigate the beliefs and innermost thoughts that are holding you back and label each one, based on actual evidence - true or false. Some thoughts might even be a mix of the two, with some of it being true and some of it untrue.

For example, let's say you uncover the limiting belief: "No design agency will ever hire me again because I'm not very good at Adobe InDesign." It is most likely not true that you will NEVER be hired again. However, if you honestly feel that you need more training in InDesign, this might be the perfect time to take a course and sharpen your skills. Self-compassion allows you to not beat yourself for not knowing this program better, but there is a constructive part of the belief: the need for additional training. It prevents this one limiting belief from festering into a "skill fail" that ends up defining you in your mind as a lesser job candidate, which can create a sense of anxiety palpable to others, including employers. This practice will help you separate the true parts of your limiting beliefs from the false parts.

Key Self-Compassion Actions

Gratitude Notes: At the end of each day, write a note to yourself detailing all the things you're grateful about from the day. This is a method of showing yourself grace and kindness, and identifying the good things you accomplished, especially when, on the surface, it might seem like your day was not successful.

Lean On Your Super Team: Make an intentional effort to receive compassion and care from other people, especially when your first instinct might be to wave them off and say, "no, I'm fine, don't worry about me." Give yourself conscious permission to allow others to offer up emotional support. And be willing to ask for help when you need it too – they aren't mind readers!

Be Patient With Yourself: The process will take its own time and pattern no matter how impatient or frustrated you get with it. Acknowledge the things you do have control over (improving your resume and interview skills, upping your networking, etc.) versus what you don't (the length of your job search).

Also, remember that time is relative and while a week might feel like a month to you, it's like a snap of the fingers to a recruiter. Stay consistent with your action plan and self-care habits to use that time productively rather than see it as empty space in which to worry. Remember – there's always tomorrow, including all the new jobs that might be posted in the morning! The market is constantly evolving and eventually it will create a space just for you. Keep the faith.

Key Points:

- **Even the strongest, most resilient people can struggle with difficult emotions during the job search. Self-compassion can act as a wall between you and the brunt of those emotions.**

- **Opening the door to self-compassion also opens the door to self-care, a powerful way of valuing your physical, mental, emotional, and spiritual needs.**

- **Raise your awareness about your self-talk – written and verbal – and ask if you would speak to a child or a friend the way you speak to yourself.**

- **Practice self-compassion with gratitude notes and regular check-ins with your Super Team, as these action steps are self-compassion in practice.**

Chapter 11

Confidence

There's a sweet spot to be found between vulnerability and overconfidence in job search. In this spot is where Career EQ lives – showing up "owning" your personal brand, with the willingness to acknowledge that you don't know what you don't know, to let people help you, and to listen to feedback.

Finding that right balance of confidence and vulnerability can affect how you process the other job search emotions while also determining how smoothly your search goes. A lack of confidence is your own worst enemy, slowing the process and muddying how you come across to others. A healthy dose of confidence can be the best tool you can ask for in your search, bolstering and adding clarity and ease to all your efforts.

How Confidence Shows Up In The Job Search

Quality Of Job Search Efforts

It goes without saying that job tactics fueled by confidence are more successful than those fueled by negative emotions. Confidence in yourself and what you can bring to a company shows up in the thoroughness and consistency of all your job search efforts, from writing a standout resume, proactively seeking out networking opportunities, to the preparation for and execution of a solid interview, all the way through to the negotiation period. When you're confident, you're more likely to highlight your strengths on paper and in person. With interviewing and negotiation especially, confidence is a two-way street. The more prepared you are, the more confident you'll be. The more confident you are in yourself, the more you'll invest in your preparation and delivery, increasing your overall odds of success.

In The Face Of Rejection

The lack of confidence can show up in the face of the uncertainty and repeated rejection inherent in the job search. The most rock solid sense of confidence can be shaken by the initial job loss. A lackluster resume and uncertain networking and interview skills can further decrease confidence. Lack of feedback on multiple resume submissions and then being rejected after multiple rounds of interviews, can make a person question their confidence.

Overconfidence

Excessive confidence can work against you. One job seeker had an impressive resume, was extremely competent and experienced in his field, and was having no problems at all booking interviews – first interviews. It was the subsequent rounds he wasn't getting called back for. He seemed to be stuck in a frustrating cycle of "don't call us we'll call you."

This candidate was feeling overly confident about himself and his odds of landing the position and later learned he wasn't answering the actual interview questions. Instead, he would go rogue and give the employers the information that *he* wanted them to know about him. Needless to say - this disregard for the interview process was not a successful strategy. (That doesn't mean, of course, that you shouldn't be prepared with key points you want to make sure to cover in an interview. Just make sure it's in the right context of the interviewer's questions). Digging deeper, it was fear of interviewing driving his odd behavior, and with some basic mock interview practice, he gained confidence and improved his interviewing success.

Being overconfident is an employer turnoff, creating an impression of egotism, low emotional intelligence, and overall unlikeability. Build up all the confidence you want, but Career EQ means keeping it in check under the surface as a quiet, powerful surge of inner strength and self-knowledge.

Tactics To Build Confidence

Refresh Your Skills

Fresh out of a top business School, Wendy worked her way up to corporate leadership positions at various Fortune 500 companies for over a decade. Then, out of the blue, her best friend from business school called her with exciting news - their "big idea" from business school finally had a shot at becoming reality. They had investors! Wendy was excited about the journey ahead and felt confident that she'd be able to apply all the business skills and knowledge she'd amassed through her high level corporate positions.

Unfortunately, after five years of blood, sweat and tears, the business venture failed and her friendship was in tatters. Wendy's confidence in her business knowledge and abilities was left severely shaken after her entrepreneurial experience.

On one hand, despite the passion she had for her business, she realized she missed her original career path: affecting change and making a positive impact at Fortune 500 companies. But on the other, she struggled with a lack of confidence stemming from the question of whether she was qualified to do so after experiencing her business failure. She looked at how much had changed in her fast-changing industry since she'd left to be an entrepreneur. She wondered if she had what it took to compete with younger candidates with fresher skill sets.

Wendy's job search action plan, therefore, centered on boosting her confidence by sharpening her skills and knowledge. Rather than sitting in worry about "the competition" we encouraged Wendy to get out there, do her homework, find out exactly what knowledge, certifications, and skills that she'd need to be competitive in her search, and acquire those things through online learning, in-person courses, certification programs and any other means necessary.

Wendy summoned her courage along with the realization that this course of action would also offer valuable networking opportunities, and went back to school. At first she was nervous, but finding herself surrounded by other professionals like herself, she began regaining her old confidence in her business skills and knowledge. Her entrepreneurial failure had nearly wiped out a key belief she'd once held about herself – "Hey, I'm REALLY good at business!" Going back to school brought it all back and by the end of her courses, her confidence had grown like gangbusters. Her next job opportunity, as a matter of fact, came from a networking lead she'd gotten from one of her classmates!

What can you be doing to refresh your skills and knowledge and give yourself a competitive edge in your search? During this time when you're between jobs, what additional certifications, courses and skills could you obtain? In addition to using them to buff up your resume, sharpening your skill set can do the same for your confidence. The self-assurance (and maybe even swagger!) you gain from your new-found skills will carry through not just on your resume but in your interview and salary negotiation as well.

Practice

Lisa was dreading the salary negotiation part of the job search the most. She'd never done this in her old line of work. But now, moving into sales, she knew this would be a key part of the process, and she was feeling less than confident in her ability to navigate it successfully.

To help build up her confidence around her self-worth, she first focused on personal brand exercises to reconnect with the value she'd be bringing to her next job and polished her resume. But the most important tactic Lisa deployed to prepare for the salary negotiation was practice. She rehearsed various ways that such a conversation could play out and put thought into how she would handle each one. She also did her market research and set her lowest, ideal, and stretch (moonshot) dollar figures and compensation packages.

Because of her preparation, Lisa was feeling confident by the time of the actual negotiations - until she received her first offer, a major lowball, beneath what she was willing to accept according to her plan. As she'd practiced, she did her best to negotiate, but the employer wouldn't budge. But Lisa was feeling confident about her worth and that she would get other opportunities and she turned the employer down. With confidence comes courage!

Lisa was absolutely right about the other opportunities, and sure enough, another offer quickly came along for much more money. With the initial offer so high, she even negotiated above her "stretch" figure *and* the job was closer to home so she had a shorter commute!

Practice might not make perfect but it almost always acts as a confidence builder. As we've talked about in previous chapters - mock interviewing, networking practice, and even visualization, can help you work out the kinks while also building emotional muscle memory around the scenario so when you're in the real situation, you'll feel confident in your performance. As we just learned, practice also extends outside of interviewing to the salary negotiation, something many job seekers struggle with. Rehearsing potential salary conversations is a big confidence builder. It's worth the extra practice because by that point in the process you've almost crossed the finish line. Why not put in the extra effort, practice negotiating to get paid your value, and finish your job search strong?

Take Control Checkpoint: Confidence Level

1. **How do you feel answering the question: "Tell me about yourself."**

2. **How confident are you in your completed resume?**

3. **How confident are you in your interviewing skills?**

4. **How confident are you in your job search overall?**

5. **What could you do better? What is one thing that could make you *more* confident?**

Set Physical Cues

Jasmine had been bouncing around in administrative assistant jobs in a variety of industries. In search of a promising career path moving forward, her coach took a look at her resume and noticed relatively minor graphic design tasks sprinkled in with otherwise purely administrative positions, so she asked her about it. Jasmine absolutely lit up at the mention of the tasks, volunteering information about her background in graphic design that she'd been nurturing for years. But unsure how she could make a living at it without a formal education in the field, she hadn't pursued any jobs in design. Even though it was a side passion, Jasmine did have a portfolio of her work, and it was extremely impressive!

With some encouragement, she decided to start pursuing marketing support and coordinator roles that might have more design opportunities than her previous administrative assistant jobs. She could see that marketing coordinator roles might be a stepping stone to full time graphic design work. But she was still having trouble summoning the confidence to see herself actually working in graphic design for a living.

To remind herself of her creative talents and increase her confidence during interviews for the marketing positions, Jasmine brought with her a rock she'd painted as a child, with a beautiful, brightly colored design. Her rock represented the first time in her life people had complimented her creative abilities. Holding and looking at it now was an instant confidence booster. The physical cue worked! Jasmine "rocked" her interview for a marketing coordinator role at a smaller company that would be able to leverage her design skills ("they even asked to see my portfolio right there on the spot!") and landed the job.

Think about a time when you felt confident in your talents, abilities, skills and overall value. What helped you create that emotional state – hitting a certain goal, listening to certain music, holding an object that made you feel confidence, reading a certain passage of a book? Tangible cues like Jasmine's rock can trigger your past memories of confidence, bringing them into the present with you. Another example would be, like many professional athletes do, listening to a certain song that boosts your confidence.

Get A Part Time Job

One way to keep your confidence up, while also creating a cushion of income and maintaining a routine and structure in your life (therefore avoiding some of the loss and paralyzing emotions), is to get a part time job while searching for your next career opportunity. A part time job, consulting on the side, or even gig work, no matter how seemingly small or insignificant, creates purpose and confidence. On top of that you might discover new skills and talents that you never knew you had, further increasing your confidence. Challenge yourself to seek a side job outside your comfort zone that stretches you as a person and a professional!

Finish Your Resume

We have noticed time and time again that once a job seeker completes their resume and the branding process, their confidence really begins to kick in. This is probably the top action you can take that exists at the intersection of "job search tactic" and "emotional processing."

Working on your personal brand and updating your resume offers the opportunity to review and reflect on your career accomplishments while ensuring that your resume matches the brand impression you're aiming for. It also allows you to see yourself in the best possible light, boosting your confidence for the search ahead. It acts as a tangible milestone that can create a ray of hope that gives you momentum and moves you forward in your job search.

The task of pulling together past successes and accomplishments holds up a confidence boosting mirror, reminding you of your value. Many a job seeker has looked at their resume and said: "Wow, I look pretty good – I'd hire me!!"

Brand Angle: A Current Resume

Is your resume a source of confidence? If you've been searching for a while now, when's the last time you updated your resume? Not just glanced at it for typos, said "good enough" and sent it along - but really looked at it closely to see how well your work history, accomplishments and goals are reflected?

Focus On What You Can Control

The quickest way to drain your self-confidence is by expending energy and worry on things beyond your control. Focusing on rejection, negative feedback, or no feedback at all feeds the little voices of self-doubt in your head – the ones telling you you're not good enough. Starve the voices by shifting your attention only to things within your control - resume, putting effort into the high value job search activities, interview practice, even your interview clothes. Wearing clothes that make you feel powerful and attractive is something within your control that is also a huge confidence builder. Finally, no matter how out of control the job search seems, you always have the opportunity to control your stress. Allowing stress to accumulate will affect your confidence levels. Things like self-care, changing your self-talk, and positive affirmations can replace stress with forward motion. All these things can remind you to exercise your power of choice which can take you out of hopelessness and into confidence.

Reconnect With Your Self-Worth

If much of your self-worth was attached to a job you no longer occupy, that blow to your identity can also be a blow to your confidence. Tap into your successes in that role, as well as a deeper awareness of who you were outside of that job, the skills, talents, and successes you had before it and additional ones you've gained because of it. What past successes can you draw on to build your confidence now? Losing a job doesn't take away the value of any of your contributions. Reconnect with all that value, draw confidence from it and use it to zoom out and see your wholeness – the complete and valuable person you are outside of your jobs. What value do you bring to a workplace, your community, and the world?

Take Control Checkpoint:
Reconnecting with Confidence

1. **Where did you find confidence in the past?**

2. **What is holding you back from feeling that confidence now?**

3. **Is there something specific that took away your confidence that you still need to work through?**

4. **Do you believe you can be confident again – why or why not?**

*If these questions being up unresolved or traumatic events, they may require additional tools such as behavioral health services (counseling, peer support groups, etc.). Do not hesitate to use additional tools and do not underestimate the emotions that you may experience.

Apply For A Stretch Position

For bonus confidence building points, stretch outside your comfort zone, find a job that you feel you really want, but might not feel fully qualified for, and go for it! Maybe you have some of the skills and experience required, but not all. If you have 60% of the qualifications, you still have a shot - especially if you can demonstrate the cultural fit and the ability to learn key skills for the job. Put your confidence to the test by selling yourself for a position just above your qualifications. Someone told me once that it's your job as a candidate to decide if you're interested in a position, and the hiring manager's job to determine if you are a fit. Even if you're not a fit for that role, there's a chance that other roles could open up at that company that would be a fit. What's the worst that could happen? What's the *best* that could happen?

Key Confidence Building Actions

Power Poses: Practice feeling confident through empowered body language like "power posing" as coined by psychologist Amy Cuddy who talks about it in her TED Talk (which I would highly encourage you to watch). An example of "power posing" would be to stand up tall, expand your body to fill the space you're in and with head held high, place your hands on your hips akin to Wonder Woman. Cuddy cites evidence through her work that this type of empowered body language creates a release of hormones that physiologically improves your mental state, naturally boosting confidence.

Practice Positivity: Surround yourself with positive people! You're more likely to create positive self-talk if your external circumstances reflect those same vibes. Positivity reaps more positivity so be cognizant of who you're spending time around and whether their words and actions are building or tearing down your confidence.

Big Picture: Try not to attach your confidence level to individual outcomes (like an application or interview rejections) but rather connect it to the big picture – your past accomplishments and overall value as an employee and a person. When you attach your confidence to an individual situation, you're more likely to end up on an unpredictable, emotional rollercoaster, making the job search all the more difficult.

Key Points:

- While a lack of confidence can make you invisible in the job search, swinging to the other end of the spectrum and exhibiting an "EQ blind" overconfidence can make you appear egotistical and out of touch to employers.

- Bolster your confidence by practicing key actions in the job search process like interviewing and salary negotiation. Also be sure your personal brand comes through in your resume as a representation of your best career self!

- Assess what has given you confidence in the past - thoughts, objects, rituals, etc. - and see how you can replicate those now.

Chapter 12

Excitement

Our last of the key Career EQ emotions, is excitement. This seemingly straightforward emotion actually wears a few faces in the job search. It's the face of victory when you finally receive an offer for your next dream job. It's also the energetic face you wear to persuade potential employers to hire you, no matter how you're feeling or how well or poorly your job search is going. But in cases of over-enthusiasm, excitement can work against you, overwhelming others and potentially sabotaging the positive first impression you're trying to make. The stories in this chapter will show you the difference and the tactics will demonstrate how to use excitement to your advantage in the job search.

How Excitement Shows Up In The Job Search

Opportunity

Excitement is an obvious emotion when you land a job, but believe it or not, exciting opportunities can also emerge from what some employers call "the gift of go" - when an employee is released out of an employment situation that is at best, not making them deliriously happy and at worst, making them miserable. Many of our clients, after processing the initial loss emotions from getting laid off, find excitement in the silver lining of being "freed" from a less-than-ideal situation. One individual excitedly told us, after being let go from a company where he'd been merely going through the motions at work.

"Instead of having my career defined for me, now I'm in this unexpected position where I get to define it myself!"

Over-Excitement

Cole saw his layoff as a blessing. He had long felt undervalued by his company and, believing the "grass was greener" outside his office walls, enthusiastically leaped into the job search, fully expecting great things to happen. He was confident that once he put his stellar resume on the market, he would be offered a better position in no time at all.

But after six months of continuously turning down lesser jobs that he felt were "beneath him," even through his excitement, Cole could see the writing on the wall. He realized that he had overestimated the market for his background and eventually did some more in depth research to get the facts so he could step into round two of his search on more solid footing. This combination of doing his homework and scaling back his excitement to see his situation more realistically, did the trick. He soon received a solid job offer from a company on his top five list.

As mentioned at the top of the chapter, showing *too* much excitement during your job search can be equally detrimental to not showing enough. This can happen at any point throughout the search but here are some specific examples to watch out for.

- When, like Cole, you get so caught up in "the grass is greener" syndrome that you overestimate the opportunities ahead of you and underestimate how challenging it will be to find your next job.
- When that first interview call comes in, you get so excited that you convince yourself the job is as good as yours and fail to adequately prepare for the interview, and in doing so, blow the opportunity.
- When you become so excited about one particular company that you oversell yourself to the recruiter, coming off more desperate than excited.

- When the interview goes so well you become convinced the actual job offer is just a formality. In reality, there are likely many qualified people interviewing for the position. Make this assumption and you're also in danger of checking out for the rest of the job search process and overlooking basic but vital steps like sending a thank you follow up.

Assume nothing, control your excitement, and stay diligent all the way until you receive a legal, binding job offer signed by all parties. Then - celebrate!

Take Control Checkpoint:
Excitement as a Job Search Positive

Use these questions as an opportunity to evaluate and reflect on your level of excitement, to ensure that it's a positive addition to your job search.

1. **Am I finding myself too devastated when I hear that I was not selected to go the next round in interviews?**
2. **Am I doing my best to prepare for each interview?**
3. **Am I vowing to do my best to understand the position and articulate my fit and value for the position, in each interview?**
4. **Am I approaching each interview with the understanding that there will be other excellent candidates and I will learn from every interview to get better?**
5. **Am I practicing relaxation techniques (like breathing exercises, journaling and meditation) to stay focused and not get over-excited?**
6. **Am I able to notice when I am getting over-excited about the search, interviews, or expectations?**

7. **Am I grounding my expectations, by discussing with others what they are seeing and experiencing in the job marketplace?**
8. **Am I getting too focused on any one opportunity, and putting myself at risk by not keeping my options open?**
9. **Am I over-talking or over-selling in my interviews? (if you've done mock interviews with your Super Team, they can give you feedback on this.)**

Tactics For Building And Managing Excitement

Write A Mantra

Emma had been laid off from her job as a reporter for a newspaper that, like many others, had gone out of business due to the changing media industry. She was extremely anxious about reentering the competitive field of journalism, especially with what she saw as a "meager little resume." Although journalism and writing had been her lifelong passions, she toyed with the idea of leaving the field entirely, starting from scratch in a new, more stable career, and snapping up any old minimum wage job to pay the bills in the meantime. The very idea of this broke her heart.

When Emma finally reviewed her portfolio of work, allowing the time and space since her layoff to offer a fresh perspective, she had to admit that she was a skilled reporter and talented writer. Right then and there, she pushed away any further thoughts of leaving journalism. Instead she enthusiastically decided to put those writing skills to work, writing a mantra for her job search.

The mantra Emma wrote was an upbeat job search mission statement of sorts, that would keep her confidence up, act as a lifeline to her purpose and passion, and create a sense of excitement, rather than dread, around her upcoming search. *I will not settle for anything less than my passion. I am worth the fight for my dreams!*

Think of specific words and messages that trigger excitement in your heart and soul when you read them. Play around with several options if needed and come up with a message that makes you the most excited when you say it out loud! Then, write down your mantra and keep it in a visible, easily accessible place (for example, an index card taped to your desk or the bathroom mirror, or in a graphic as the background image on your phone or computer) so you can tap into that excitement as needed.

Interpersonal Interaction

George, a long time benefits coordinator at a top health insurance company, felt like his career was finally nearing the finish line. Already in his late fifties, retirement and all its benefits were practically around the corner. In the meantime, already an introverted person by nature, he'd made it a habit to keep his head down, dashing from his car directly to his cubicle every morning, doing the work that was required of him, and avoiding contact with others as much as possible. Frankly, after working at the same company around most of the same people for decades, George was bored with the idea of socializing. So he kept his eye on the prize. He could almost taste that pension!

He hadn't counted on his company undergoing a massive reorganization due to changes in the health insurance laws. George was blindsided by the layoff – and extremely angry too, especially since he felt backed into a corner with few to no options to build a future on. He was far from excited about searching for a new job, especially this late in his career.

Nevertheless, needing to replace his income he begrudgingly delved into the job search process. It was when he reached the networking piece though, that everything shifted.

Despite all past behavior to the contrary, George found the live interaction with different people than the ones he'd been around for the last thirty or so years, to be refreshing and even exciting! From local Chamber of Commerce mixers to business luncheons, George thrived on the conversations with people he'd never met, sharing laughs, stories - and contact information. Stepping outside his cubicle walls he began seeing new options for his future outside of his prior job and the healthcare industry. He was having so much fun and learning so many new things, as a matter of fact, that he temporarily forgot he was looking for a job. So when a lucrative offer in a different industry with a higher salary and better benefits came along via one of his new networking friends – well that was the most exciting moment of all!

No matter how you're feeling, make it a priority to take your job search into the light of day and give it some air. As George learned, being around other human beings is sometimes just the emotional trigger needed to pull yourself out of the job search doldrums and into excitement about future possibilities.

In addition to traditional networking, you can also engage with other people by taking part in hobbies, volunteer work, and even branching out your job search strategy to include employer visits to companies you're interested in working at by meeting people that work at those organizations. And you never know when the hiring manager might be feeling generous and agree to meet with you if you happen to be around the corner! Have a business card and resume on hand just in case the situation should arise.

Practice Gratitude

Jeffrey was boarding a plane to Miami along with his college buddies for a reunion weekend when one of them asked him about a recent set of job interviews he'd had at a company. "Nailed 'em!" he told his friend with a big smile, completely confident that he had. The day before was the final of three interviews that had all gone very well. He was sure that by Monday when he returned, he would have a new voicemail offering him the job.

By the end of the following week though, with no word from the company, Jeffrey was perplexed and worried. What was happening here? Everything about all three of the interviews told him he was a perfect fit for the company *and* the position - the hiring manager had even said as much in the final one! After reviewing the events with Jeffrey we uncovered a potential problem - he'd failed to send a thank you note follow up.

This might not sound like the life or death of the job search, but in this case, Jeffrey had mentioned to the hiring manager that he was entertaining offers from several other companies too. We brought up the possibility that perhaps this company was waiting for a thank you note, simply to let them know they were his choice. Slightly bewildered but agreeable, Jeffrey immediately sat down and sent off a thank you email to the hiring manager. Later that same day, they called and offered him the position. As we suspected - they had been waiting for his follow up to indicate his interest.

There are two aspects to this tactic. First, and the moral of Jeffrey's story - don't get so over excited that you forget the crucial last step in your job search, the thank you follow up. The other aspect reframes the purpose of the follow up. After you've been rejected for a job, as a way of processing your temporary grief over the loss and moving back toward excitement, send a follow-up note to the employer thanking them for taking the time to meet with you and telling you about the company, introducing you to other team members, and asking them to please keep you in mind for future opportunities at the company and potentially any feedback they are willing to share with you.

This one simple gesture not only helps you move through the emotions around the temporary rejection more quickly, but it also creates forward momentum and goodwill with that company.

Balance Excitement With Self-Awareness

Lana was well aware that when she got over excited, especially about a career opportunity, her enthusiasm could be off-putting to others. She felt, however, that her enthusiasm was core to who she was and her personal brand, so she didn't want to temper this aspect of her personality. She realized this mindset might lead to a longer job search, but because of her confidence in herself and thorough understanding of her personal brand, she made the conscious choice that she'd rather be patient and wait a little longer, than compromise who she was and her core values.

Unlike many other job applicants who don't possess this level of self-awareness, during job searches when she found herself making it all the way to the interview phase and then losing out to another candidate, she did not allow herself to get frustrated. Instead, she shifted her perspective to see the rejection as an opportunity, a "sign" that the right fit was right around the corner!

Making this tactic work is incredibly dependent on the work you've done on your personal brand. This level of confidence, patience, and belief that the right fit will come along, comes from the self-awareness of who you are as a person, your gifts, what you have to offer an organization, and your goals.

Focus On Future Opportunities

Perhaps you're finding it challenging to let go of your prior job, stuck in the emotions of having such a "perfect" situation ripped away from you. As long as you're grieving your last job, it will be hard to generate excitement for your next job opportunity. Consider the possibility that you might be looking at your last job through rose colored glasses. Was it really as ideal as you thought it was or are you romanticizing it?

Here's one way to get a more accurate picture. Grab a piece of paper, and draw a line down the middle to create two side-by-side lists. On the left side, write down all the things you liked about your last job, how it aligned with your core values and personal mission, skills and talents it helped you develop, and all the future opportunities it afforded you to grow your career. What's missing from this list that you might possibly be able to find at your next job? Focusing on future career opportunities rather than obsessing about what you've lost, will help you process the grief of losing your last job and generate excitement about what is yet to come!

Key Excitement Building Actions

Exciting Activities: Make a list of things that make you excited - books, movies, spending time with certain people, specific sports, leisure, or self-care activities, spending time with nature, etc. Make it a point to incorporate as many of these activities as reasonably possible into your schedule.

The Best Medicine: Laughter is a natural energy enhancer that sends endorphins – "happy chemicals" – coursing through your body. When you're in need of an emotional pick-me-up, find a way to add some humor to your day, whether by watching a funny movie, or better yet, connecting with friends to experience that irreplaceable live and in person spontaneous humor that being around friends offers.

Get Moving: Exercise, preferably the vigorous type, is another natural chemical boost for your brain and body that helps elevate your mood and lighten things up. In the name of self-care and mood boosting hormones - get moving on a regular basis!

Visualization: Generate excitement about future possibilities by researching companies you'd like to work for, reading employee reviews, looking at company photos and engaging on their social media, and imagining yourself working there. Visualization, to the brain, creates the same mental effect as the actual experience of something.

Celebrate: Reinforce excitement positively as it happens by celebrating your job search victories!

Key Points:

- **Overexcitement can reflect negatively on your first impression and therefore act as a detriment to your success. One way to ward against it is to ground all your expectations in facts and reality.**

- **Feeling less than excited about yourself and your potential? Write a mantra that fires you up about both!**

- **Consider the possibility that continuing to grieve your prior job (and the possibilities it once held in your mind) might be the thing holding you back from truly becoming excited about your career future and the job search that will get you there.**

Part V

Career EQ 2.0

"We cannot tell what may happen to us in the strange medley of life. But we can decide what happens in us — how we can take it, what we do with it — and that is what really counts in the end."
— Joseph Fort Newton

Chapter 13

Career EQ on the job

The lessons gained through implementing Career EQ are not isolated to the job search or even the workplace. The ability to *notice*, *understand*, and *process* your emotions is more critical to success and happiness today more than ever before. Some might attribute this newfound focus on emotional intelligence to the younger generations who have entered the workforce and shown through their example, the value of empathy and emotional authenticity. These elements and other emotional management principles are now embedded in school curriculums and youth culture in ways that previous generations never experienced, sometimes making young people seem hyper-sensitive at times. I personally see this as a good thing. Prioritizing emotional intelligence is a net positive not just at work but in all areas of your life.

When you commit to developing your emotional intelligence the same way you would any other on-the-job skills, it can be the "X Factor" that makes you stand out from your peers, relate better to your coworkers, bosses, and subordinates, weather stress and everyday conflict better, and level up in your career. Let's look at some different areas where Career EQ as well as some of the other key job search tactics we've covered, can work to your advantage *beyond* the job search.

Weathering Stress

Has what you've learned in this book uncovered any emotional triggers for you? Be aware that the emotions that surface during your job search, might be the very same ones that rear their heads again during other career-related stress situations.

For instance, if getting "unjustly" terminated from your last job sparked feelings of anger for you, be aware that unfair scenarios in future jobs - like a coworker getting a promotion you felt you were better qualified for - might have the same effect. This might not seem like a big deal (or may even seem fairly obvious) but having this awareness and the tactics for dealing with anger from a Career EQ standpoint could prevent you from acting impulsively and potentially damaging your reputation and your future.

Maybe the overwhelming frustration you felt while staring into the "black hole" of resumes, tossing in one after another but receiving no feedback in return, might come up again in the form of not getting any feedback about your performance from your next supervisor. The denial you dealt with in the job search as a result of believing there was no room for improvement in your interviewing skills might be costing you an opportunity in your current position where learning a new skill to overcome a weakness might allow you to level up. How many parallels can you find between the emotions you felt during your job search and how the lessons and tactics you learned to deal with them, can benefit you now on the job?

Pay particular attention to "who you are" when you're stressed. Most of us can be calm, enthusiastic, and productive under fair weather and blue skies. But it's under storm clouds where the true tests of character, judgment, coping skills, and professionalism, occur. Making it a priority to master your Career EQ offers a level of protection in those situations. This is a perfect opportunity to leverage feedback you've received from your Super Team to help you know yourself better going forward. And keep that Super Team in your hip pocket, because you never know when their counsel can be helpful again.

Uncover your emotional patterns and master your tactics for dealing with them now and avoid potentially messy cleanup work later. This mastery of Career EQ will give you a competitive advantage in every single job you have for the rest of your life, along with many situations outside of work as well!

Your Brand Promise

When you applied for your new job, you made a certain brand promise about who you are and what you could contribute to the organization. Now it's time to deliver (or better, over-deliver) on that promise, and build a reputation for yourself and your brand that lives up to how you sold yourself. From day one, begin building a case for yourself - both through your performance and your attitude - so six months down the line when your supervisor evaluates whether she's happy that she hired you - the answer is a resounding yes. Then, after that, continue building on your brand and your value, positioning yourself for the next role down the road, and then the one after that and so on.

Take Control Checkpoint: Keeping Your Promise

Are you delivering on your brand promise? Do this simple exercise and see.

1. **Keep track of your accomplishments. It's easier to do this on a regular basis than trying to remember everything over the course of the year. This is a great habit to get into whether it's helpful for performance review time or for the next time you update your resume.**

2. **Revisit what you learned about personal branding earlier in the book including the questions you answered in Chapter 2 to help you get clear on your own brand. Think of each piece of your brand as a promise you've made to your current employer.**

3. **Now pull out the job description and duties of your current role. How can you connect the dots between your accomplishments, your brand and your current job description? How can you ensure you are following through on the promise you made to your employer?**

For example, imagine a piece of your brand is: "possesses great creativity & innovation" and a part of your job description involves presenting at least one new idea to your supervisor each month. As someone who leads with the promise of creativity and innovation, wouldn't that be something you'd want to consistently over-deliver on (thereby gaining attention in the process)?

Resume

We saw that in many of our stories, how the simple act of updating their resume created an energetic shift in people's job searches, transforming their emotional state from feelings of loss or paralysis to one of forward momentum and enthusiasm. Why wait until your next job search to dust off your resume and start from square one to update it? One of the strongest parts of a resume is your accomplishments, so why not write about them while the details and pride in what you've done, are still fresh in your mind? This might not necessarily mean pulling out your resume the same day of that big promotion or award, but maybe a month later versus years later when the specifics of the event aren't as fresh or exciting to write about anymore. Accomplishments aside, it's generally a good idea to update your resume once a year.

Social Media

By now, you've spent a good deal of time and energy in building your personal brand online, especially on social media. Even if being on *LinkedIn* is not critical to your day to day job, keep your profile active by posting updates or interesting content and stay in touch with your connections on a regular basis. Build and maintain those relationships now so when it comes time for your next job search, you're not placed in the uncomfortable position of reaching out to people you haven't spoken to in an awkwardly long period of time and asking for their help.

For Women In Business

The networking skills that presumably helped you land your current position are the same ones that will help propel you up the job ladder, over and over, for the duration of your career. Networking will help you connect to and build relationships with people in high places that can help advance your career.

This is especially key for women in the workplace to remember. Research has shown that many women do not apply for the jobs they really want. But for women in leadership roles (or those with goals to get there) the ability to actively network, build corporate visibility, and proactively go for those jobs, can be a career accelerator. The inability to do this can cause careers to stall and even stagnate.

Most common for women is to overlook the corporate visibility piece of their internal networking efforts. We define this as getting to know the right people in your organization who are influential in making promotion (or other critical) decisions.

In addition to corporate visibility, two other factors to focus on in your networking and career advancement efforts are your personal effectiveness and business acumen. These are three areas we focus on as career accelerators for women. These are also relevant for men, of course, we just tend to see the need for women to be more intentional in these areas.

For instance, it's common to prioritize personal effectiveness, which means how well you're doing in your job. It's slightly less common, however, for women to actively sharpen their business acumen by asking themselves questions like: How well do you know the business of the business? Are you well-versed in how the company makes money and understanding the strategic aspects of the organization? If you had the opportunity to sit down for lunch with the CEO or CFO of your company, could you hold your own?

We hear women talking about wanting "a seat at the table" all the time. Well, we were working with a woman who realized through her coaching, that at important meetings she literally chose *not* to take a seat at the conference table. Instead, she would intentionally choose to sit in one of the chairs on the periphery of the crowded room. As a result, she never felt like she fully had a voice in the meetings or that her ideas mattered. We helped her see that these seemingly small decisions you make, like where you sit in meetings, make an impact on how you're interacting with and impacting other people. At the next meeting, she made the decision to sit *at* the table and it changed everything – how she felt about herself, her confidence, and her ability to contribute during the meeting. Now, several months and many meetings later, this woman behaves differently not just at meetings, but throughout her job. People have started treating her differently because she now exudes the confidence that was initially triggered by her decision that day to actually take a seat at the table.

This type of confidence carries over to all aspects of corporate visibility, including the courage to speak up and ask others to advocate for you. I often say that women are over mentored and under sponsored. What is the distinction between the two? A mentor imparts wisdom about your industry, corporate culture, and other broad topics generally pertinent to your overall career. Mentoring is usually a comfortable experience for women especially, as much of it is centered around learning, connecting, and setting goals. There are some comfort zone challenges, but more than anything, a mentor helps to remind you of your value.

A sponsor, on the other hand, reminds *others* of your value. Their role is to bring up your name specifically to people in power when opportunities for promotions come up. Finding a sponsor to advocate on your behalf like this, requires a clear understanding of your (brand) value and bold ability to speak up about it without hesitation or apology.

How are you making sure the right people know who you are and what you're capable of, so when the right opportunity comes up, they confidently think of you and put their own name on the line by recommending you? How do you intentionally make sure that you're building relationships with people who understand your career ambitions enough that you can ask them to keep their eyes peeled for available opportunities for you and potentially even go to bat for you?

One woman I know is excellent at this! Early on in her career at a male dominated organization, she impressed a senior male colleague with her work and she made an effort to stay in touch. Before she knew it, he began calling her asking if she was going to apply for this position or that one. Behind the scenes, he was advocating for her. She continued to rise in the organization, and she called to tell him one day that she'd be applying for one of the top positions in the company to which he responded, "I was waiting for you to call and tell me!" Being proactive like this, is next level networking!

This issue is a deep and complex social evolution with terrific research and many books that can illustrate it further. If this is of interest, I suggest you search for other resources on the topic of gender in the workplace and explore more.

A Positive Difference

Did you know that having a good job is crucial to your overall happiness? This has been proven by the Gallup organization on multiple occasions as well as the inverse of this, that having a job you do *not* like contributes to unhappiness and overall dissatisfaction with life.

My hope for you is that you will use the information, stories, and techniques in this book to successfully land your next role - one that inspires you, makes you happy, is a great fit for you, and allows you to use your gifts and goals to grow and be successful in your career.

Because, when you have a good job and you're succeeding in it there is a ripple effect to all other areas and aspects of your life. You're going to come home and be a better spouse, a better parent, a better friend, and a better citizen in the community. That ripple effect, will truly make a positive difference in the world!

Conclusion

During the writing of *Take Control of Your Job Search!* I found myself struggling with one of the strongest and scariest emotions in this book - fear. A serious situation came up at work that if not handled properly could have had significant implications for my company. Without going into detail about the issue, I found myself feeling a deep sense of fear in the pit of my stomach about what this could mean for the company. In my mind the idea of losing clients, revenue, and even our reputation was weighing heavily on me. If you've worked in leadership in any organization, you may be able to relate to this. Like a natural disaster, this event appeared out of nowhere and turned business-as-usual right on its head.

Even walking into the security of my home and the comfort of being around my family didn't help what I was feeling. At night, I would lie awake swimming in fear. I felt paralyzed at work - all the while hoping the growing sense of dread in my stomach would somehow go away on its own. Even while realizing, especially after writing this book, that it probably would not because that's not how emotions work. I spoke with my husband and parents (members of my own Super Team), but it was hard to see beyond my emotional fog.

In the midst of one of my 3 a.m. wakeups, I reflected deeply on the fear emotion. I knew that if left unchecked and unprocessed, it could create a physical and mental chain reaction that would impact my personal and work life, my productivity, focus, along with affecting everyone around me at the office and at home. Then, suddenly, I thought: Take Control! How could I use the tactics I *just* wrote about in this book to deal with the fear currently paralyzing me? I pulled up the fear chapter and flipped to the tactics section, and realized I had everything I needed right at my fingertips!

The main tactic I deployed was asking the question - "What's the worst that could happen and what would I do if it did?" I grabbed a notebook and started scribbling. Feeling a little better and more in control of my fear, I decided to take the exercise further, asking myself even more questions: How could I keep those bad things from happening at all? What proactive measures could I take now? What are the likely consequences of the situation vs. the worst case scenario that I was creating in my head? If the worst case scenario happened . . . would I be okay, my company, employees and family? Would we all get past this situation? The more I wrote in the notebook, the better I felt. My breath and pulse slowed and I began to think more clearly. I began feeling more like myself again. While I can't say that all the fear went away, I was able to see the situation with greater perspective so I could have greater control over the emotion instead of it controlling me.

This incident confirms the message you just read in the prior chapter - that Career EQ is effective in *any* situation where emotions threaten to overtake you - job search, work, or personal! You can walk into virtually any life scenario involving runaway emotions armed with these tactics, and you will have the upper hand.

That's why I decided, rather than isolating each set of emotion tactics to their respective chapters, that I would also compile them in an easy-to-reference appendix that follows. I want you to have the same easy access to these tactics that I did on that recent fearful night. The best knowledge is the kind that you can apply.

Emotions are a universal truth that transcend country, culture, ethnicity, age, socioeconomic status, education, religion, gender, and all the other ways we tend to separate ourselves. We *all* have emotions, we *all* experience them in our own way, and we *all* have times when they get the best of us. But with proven ways of dealing with those emotions at our fingertips - the world can seem a little less scary and out of control.

Take Control – Choose Success!

Lauren

.

Appendix A

Tactics Guide

Loss Emotions

Grief & Sadness

Work on Your Personal Brand and Update Your Resume:
Updating your resume offers the opportunity to review and reflect on your career accomplishments while ensuring that your resume matches the personal brand impression you're aiming for. It also allows you to see yourself in the best possible light, boosting your confidence for the search ahead. It acts as a tangible milestone that can create a ray of hope that gives you momentum and moves you forward in your job search!

Get Closure: It's important to acknowledge and value the relationships formed in your old job. Take stock, decide who you wish to stay connected to and at the same time, which relationships have run their course and therefore deserve a proper goodbye.

Don't Deny It: You might be tempted to rush directly from the job loss to the search for your next job, ignoring your emotions by taking action with the mindset, "okay, I lost my job, I've got to find a new one, let's move on." You might need to move forward quickly, but don't do so at the risk of the healthy processing of grief which can therefore be a big obstacle to your job search. Recognize and honor the loss you've just gone through - don't deny its reality.

Let It Out: Grieving is the process of looking back on and honoring what you once had. Therefore, and this is a common theme throughout the book, writing down your feelings is paramount in "unpacking" the complete experience - what you had (the job) and your feelings about losing it. Write it down, acknowledge it, say goodbye to it, even write a letter to yourself about what you learned and what you want to do differently in your next job. Journaling is one of the most valuable tools available for processing grief as well as all the other emotions in this book.

No Apologies: Accept the fact that you are grieving a loss just like any other and don't feel obligated to apologize to others as you go through what is a very normal process of grieving. Don't try to rush the process simply to appear "okay" or to appease others who might have a different timeline in mind for grieving a job loss (whether based on their own experience or maybe they've never lost a job so they don't understand).

Take Action, However Small: While honoring your grieving process and giving yourself the time and space you need, it's also important to take action, even in a small way, to avoid getting stuck in this emotion (thus halting your job search). Small actions to move you forward might be watching webinars, reading books, or listening to podcasts, either about the job search or relating to your industry.

It's like the flywheel analogy, described by Jim Collins in his book *Good to Great*. It takes great effort to push a heavy flywheel into motion, but as you keep pushing, even in small bursts, the wheel goes faster and faster. Eventually, the flywheel is able to create its own momentum and spins on its own.

Each action you take toward your next job search, even when it's the last thing you want to do and no matter how small, will contribute to that overall momentum. Keep pushing, even a little at a time! Creating clear action steps as part of an action plan, will help you shift your energy from sadness to forward momentum. Taking action will also give you space to acknowledge and process your emotions in a healthy way.

Find Something You Can Control: One way to soften the blow of the job loss and subsequent separation grief, is to find something you CAN control about the process. For instance, cleaning out your desk or setting aside time to say goodbye to your coworkers. Anything that you decide to take action on that moves you forward is taking back the control in your job search.

Seek Out New Opportunities: Try reframing the loss of a job as an opportunity to broaden your horizons. Is there a passion you've never pursued that you can turn into a career? Perhaps this is the beginning of your "encore career" - something you've always wanted to do but never had time to before now, something less demanding and for many of you "less corporate" than your job. This might be coaching sports at the local high school, or becoming self-employed or working in your same field in an industry you love such as music or sports. Or you might be drawn toward making a positive impact via work in the nonprofit sector or perhaps going back to school for an advanced degree. The opportunities, once you zoom out from the acute state of separation and loss, are truly endless!

Anger

Turn It Into Words: Anger in particular is an emotion that can be destructive to yourself and your search if you allow it to simmer and boil internally. Give it space to breathe by putting it into words - whether verbally to support people in your life, or in writing via journaling. Use your words to direct harmful negative energy into productive positive progress.

Rewrite Your Self-Talk: Anger can easily turn into a toxic, progress-thwarting emotion. One of its offshoots, like a hurricane spinning off tornadoes, can be negative self-talk, which destroys your self-confidence from the inside out. Nip it in the bud by first, being aware of any negative thoughts invading your consciousness and then by using positive affirmations to rewrite it on the spot before it does any damage!

Ask yourself, "Where is my anger really coming from? Is it still from the initial lay off? Have I fully processed that? Or is it from the current rejections I'm getting while looking for a new job? Am I more angry at other people or myself?" Identify the source of the anger you're currently experiencing.

Next, write down the inner dialogue in your head, especially during the challenging pieces of the job search like when you're getting rejections. For example, "I'm not smart enough to get this job."

Then, look at what you've written down, these things you're saying to yourself, and ask: "How is this useful? How is this thinking serving me and my purpose? How can I change these thoughts so they help me move forward?"

Get The Facts: Nothing in a job search is personal. Therefore, if you're finding yourself in a resentful space and feel like you are taking the rejection personally, assign yourself the research project of making sure you've got your facts straight. Analyze market pay in your region, assess your value in a position based on education and experience, what are the key requirements in the jobs you're applying for, and look at other aspects of organizations you're applying to, like benefits, culture, and management styles. The more data you have to support your efforts, the stronger your overall position will be in your search. This research will also help you get clear on your core values and what it is you're looking for.

In a job search and especially a negotiation, facts are your friends. Do your homework as early in your search as possible, researching your industry and the market in general to arm yourself with the right information to use as the foundation of your job search action plan.

Don't Take It Personally: Getting let go from your job is not personal, despite how it may feel. The sooner you can get into this mindset the better. On the other side of this is buying into the belief that you do have the skills to take to the open market where you'll be valued. Then you can start taking forward steps in your job search.

Venting: It's hard to hide strong anger in a job interview, so make sure you have an outlet for this. Give yourself sufficient time and space to vent. If you're more of an introvert, "venting" might mean journaling. If you're an extrovert, you might need to seek out people you trust and build a "Super Team" and blow off steam verbally to them. If the anger you're feeling is too strong to be resolved by those methods, you might consider delaying your job search even further, and giving yourself time to seek an outside resource like a counselor.

Write a Letter: Write a letter to your former employer - to your old boss, or to the CEO or owner. Direct your feelings to the person that you hold responsible for your current situation. Read it aloud like you are saying the words to their face. You might even want to yell certain parts of the letter to them! Then you can go through the cathartic process of disposing of the letter. Do NOT send it! Burn it in your fireplace, or if that isn't an option, you can send it down the garbage disposal. This process is helpful to then let go of the anger. You got it out of your system, so now you can start to move on without the burden of that anger.

Personal Coping Strategies: Tap into your self-awareness when you're not in a state of anger and put together a set of strategies that you know will be helpful when you are angry. These could include meditation, prayer, exercise, arts and crafts, listening to certain music, taking a walk outside, more physical sports like boxing, tennis, or martial arts, or through the emotionally primal but often powerful act of having a good cry.

The key is to know which strategies work for you and lean into them when you need them. We all have emotions and it's important to set aside time to give a voice to them. Whether that means introspectively through writing or externally through physical activity, set aside time to let them have their say. If you don't, they may pop up at the most inopportune moments in your job search.

Physicality: Next time you're feeling angry, take note of your body. For many people, emotions like anger look very contracted, with the person sitting slumped down in their chair with arms crossed in front of them, fists clenched, their chest is closed, shoulders hunched up, and their head dropped down with eyes gazing at the ground. Try physically reversing this effect by standing up, unclenching your fists, putting your hands on your hips, opening your chest, putting your shoulders down, lifting up your head, and gazing straight ahead. If you can, go outside, take your shoes and socks off and connect your feet with the earth for a powerful grounding and calming effect. Make a note of how this changes the way your body feels, your emotions, and even the thoughts (self talk) in your head!

Fear

Get Professional Support: If you suspect that your fear (or panic, anxiety, or other emotion) is coming from a deeper issue or pain than the transition of job search, getting professional support in the form of counselling might be a very valuable and important step. Dealing with emotions are complicated in the best of circumstances, and with the pressure of a job search, this step might be the key to being able to clear your head and clear the air to find the right path forward.

Update Your Resume: Updating your resume is one of the single most emotionally uplifting tactics you can execute during your job search - no matter which emotion you are struggling with, and where you are in your search. In this case, reviewing your resume with fresh eyes and aligning it with your personal brand can lessen some of the fear by helping to remind you of the great work you've done in the past.

Mock Interviews: This is a tactic any job seeker can deploy to dissolve fears around interviewing, whether you have a coach or not. Enlist the help of your spouse, family member, or friend and give them a list of standard job interview questions (if you're at a loss - check the internet!). Make sure to practice the interview virtually via webcam, since that's how many job interviews these days are done, in addition to in person and phone.

In addition to providing you feedback on how you answer the questions and how you come across overall, also ask them to weigh in on how you're dressed, lighting, backdrop and anything else they notice that an interviewer might key in on as well. The key to this tactic is repetition. Practice, practice, practice! Do as many mock/virtual job interviews as needed until you feel prepared and confident.

Visualization: Don't let the associations with the "self help/ new age" world fool you. Visualization is an extremely powerful tool in fighting fear in the job search, especially in the most commonly feared stage of it, as we've discussed, interviewing. The more specificity you can include in your visualization the better. Walk your mind through the entire process of the job interview, from the moment you wake up in the morning, all the way to walking in the door, shaking the interviewer's hand, through the interview, responding to key questions, to walking out of the building afterward with head held high, feeling completely confident about the experience that has just unfolded. Picture what you'll wear down to the most minute details like shoes and jewelry, how you'll answer each question, imagine feeling calm yet energized during the entire interview, and visualize the smiles of approval from the interviewer - let no detail go unnoticed.

Go through this visualization as many times as you need until you feel the fear associated with the interview begin to melt away. Practice dealing with your fears during your visualization so your body and mind will have memorized how to respond during the actual event.

"How old is that fear?" When assessing and processing each of your job search fears, ask yourself this question, and journal about what comes up. At what age do you first recall any variation of this current fear? For example, if you're afraid of job interviewing, maybe you trace it back to a humiliating public speaking incident at age 12, making the answer to "how old is that fear?" - "12 years old." Once you've made that connection, you'll have gained the awareness (a very powerful tool in itself!) to separate out your 12 year old public speaking fear with your current adult interviewing fear and work from there. (And important to note is that if your childhood fear stems from a more serious incident and is disrupting your adult

life beyond your job search, I would urge you to please seek out professional help.)

Imagine the Worst Case Scenario (and Plan For It): First - name your worst fear (as pertaining to your job loss). For some, simply stating your fear out loud will be enough. Saying the words out loud will be enough to make you realize that your fear will most likely not come true.

But if that's not the case, the next step is to picture the worst possible thing that could happen if that fear became reality. What would be the most devastating thing that could happen if this fear came true? Imagine how you would feel, physically and mentally. Make the vision as real and detailed as possible. Now plan in concrete terms what you would do, how you would respond if this thing actually happened. How would you take care of yourself and your loved ones? How would you carry on? Once you have your plan in place, accept this worst case scenario as a possibility. Then acknowledge that you are prepared to deal with it. Finally, release this "worst case" fear with gratitude for the lessons and preparation it has brought and shift your attention back to more positive, desirable outcomes to your situation.

Where's the Evidence? When it comes to busting some of those "worst case scenario" fears, one quick and actionable fear busting technique is to ask the question - "Where's the evidence?" What actual data is there that has caused you to come to the conclusion that this awful thing is certain to happen? Our minds, especially when gripped with a strong emotion like fear, are highly irrational. Pull out of the emotional spiral by identifying what's real versus what your mind has conjured up as such. Forcing yourself to seek evidence, will uncover some of the limiting beliefs, gremlin voices, and self-doubts that are feeding your fears. Remember, even though it might hit us where it hurts – money, dignity, sense of self, and professional identity – a job loss is not personal, despite what your emotions would have you believe.

Own It: Rather than trying to ignore your fears, repress them, or deny them - own the experience of being afraid, fully. "Feel into" the experience of being afraid, physically and mentally. This is also where the technique of belly breathing, slow deep breaths originating from your abdomen, can be beneficial to release the fears that you've voluntarily "owned" and brought up to the surface.

Branding Exercise: When you're in a state of fear, it's tempting to want to run away from it, especially since with fear you're in the physiological state of "fight, flight or freeze." Flight can seem like the easiest and best option. In the job search, flight can mean, as mentioned earlier, procrastinating from getting started in your search, Or, it can show up as rushing in too quickly without processing your emotions first or outlining a strategic plan of action. A branding exercise is a positive and productive way to tap the brakes, allow some space to process your emotions, and at the same time gain clarity on your career gifts and goals. It can also serve as a reminder that you are *so* much more than this one event in your life and you have a ton to offer as a professional and as a person.

Paralyzing Emotions

Denial

Lean On Your Super Team: Denial is nearly always a symptom of a greater pain, in this case, often shame. Once you're able to uncover that truth, you'll be positioned to address it at its core and move through it. There is also a strong lesson here about not going it alone. You might be able to process some aspects of these emotions by yourself, but most require some level of support, whether from a spouse, or other loved one, a close friend, or even an outside coach or professional. If you find that denial is holding you back from admitting you need help, find the courage to lean on your super team. There's no need to suffer in silence.

Job Search Action Plan: This day-to-day plan contains specific actions that you can take continuously to move your job search forward. Keep it in a notebook, a Word document, spreadsheet, project management application or otherwise, as long as it keeps you moving forward, one step at a time. The most successful tool will be the one that you check in with and use daily.

Pieces of Your Job Search Action Plan:

1. Set a deadline for writing/editing your Resume/CV.
2. Generate a list of target companies you'd like to work for.
3. Meet with one person every week that has a direct connection to someone at one of your target companies.
4. Research the labor markets and jobs in your industry.
5. Create your social media plan - which networks will you use (presumably mainly but not exclusively LinkedIn), what time(s) of day will you go on them and for which specific tasks (to avoid mindlessly scrolling through your feeds)?
6. Develop a networking event plan - where you will search for events, how often you'd like to attend events, and your plan of action for each one (Will you need business cards? How many? Have you prepared your elevator pitch?).

7. Approach friends and other trusted contacts about scheduling mock/virtual interviews to hone your interviewing skills and presence.

Diversify Your Strategy & Seek Tough Love: It's important to diversify your job search strategy. Don't put all your eggs in one basket thereby drastically limiting your options.

Next, ask yourself: Are you looking at your situation realistically? Or is the lens of your thinking clouded by emotion, especially if you were laid off recently? One way to tell is by looking for actual hard evidence to back up your beliefs about your situation.

Finally - if needed, don't be afraid to seek out tough love. Turn to your "super team" for this - friends and family members whom you trust to have your best interests in mind to tell you constructive truths that will move you out of denial and back into the game.

Dig Deep: When you say something out loud or write it down, it sounds a lot less scary than when it's bouncing around in your head. As always, journaling is an extremely effective activity for processing emotions like denial, allowing you to get the thoughts in your head onto the page where they're almost always less confusing and overwhelming.

Start with an all-purpose brain dump and from there, begin asking yourself probing questions to bring your situation into focus. Identify any irrational beliefs you're holding about your situation (ex. Being unemployed means your loved ones are looking down on you, if you don't find a job quickly you might end up homeless, etc.).

The act of journaling, freeing your thoughts from your head onto the page, will help slow down the events happening around you, see the big picture more objectively and intellectually, and move you out of emotional overwhelm. Getting clear on what's actually happening and how you feel about it, will also give you the confidence to move forward and take intentional action in your job search.

Celebrate Your Wins: Like anything that matters in life a successful job search is a marathon not a sprint. Celebrating your wins, no matter how small, and doing it consistently, creates positive momentum tactically *and* emotionally, getting you "unstuck" from emotions that aren't moving you forward.

Moments of personal celebration and self-acknowledgment can also act as rest stops, places to breathe and reboot and refocus along the way, especially in a longer, drawn out job search. There are no wins too small for acknowledgment!

Frustration

High Value Activities: At the root of frustration is an inability to decide what to do next, and sheer overwhelm at the amount (or perceived amount) of options in front of you. This is when it's helpful to ask yourself: What is the SINGLE most valuable action I can take right now to move my job search forward? Think of the Pareto Principle, also known as the "80/20 rule" - where 20% of your actions will produce 80% of your results. Do an honest analysis matching up your actions to your outcomes, make a list of the "20%" activities creating the most and best results, and ensure they are central to your job action plan!

Energy Management: Assess where you're spending your time and energy in your day and week. The things you're doing first in your day and devoting the most time and energy too, are clearly your priorities. Actions speak louder than words. Take an honest look at what those things are. If your job search is not included among them, and you're not getting the results you want, then it's time to do some reevaluating and consider which activities you can put on the back burner for now. Just as there are so many hours in a day, there is a limit to the physical and mental energy you have available every day.

To avoid getting stuck in frustration, do an honest assessment of where you're investing your time and energy. See what needs to change to prioritize your job search, while realizing that this might require some tough decisions and saying "no" to things you normally enjoy (for the time being).

Be Authentic: In job interviews, there are certain answers you can prepare for in advance, but what you can't practice, is being yourself. That needs to come naturally because hiring managers are not just assessing whether your resume, knowledge, and experience are a fit for the organization - they're looking at whether YOU as a human being are!

Throw Yourself a Party: This is a tactic that can be used with any of the Loss and Paralyzing emotions - throw yourself a "pity party." What is your very favorite indulgence when you're feeling low? For one client stuck in frustration with her search, it was putting on a pair of comfy bunny slippers she'd had for so many years that one of the bunnies was missing an ear, and eating freshly baked chocolate chip cookies. Our coach gave her permission to throw herself a 24 hour "bunny slippers and cookies" party where she wasn't expected to do any job search activities. At the end of those 24 hours though, she would be expected to end the party, let go of her frustration and get back to work (on the job search).

Self-Reflection: As with any emotion, it would be highly unlikely that you've never felt the way you're feeling now, ever before in your life. Therefore, grab your journal and think back to all the various times you've felt frustrated in your life - whether from not getting something you wanted (or thought you wanted), feeling unable to move out of a negative situation, or otherwise. How did you move out of frustration in those times? Did you develop any coping mechanisms or strategies for dealing with your emotions that perhaps until now you've forgotten about?

Develop a Realistic Plan: When you're stuck in frustration is not the time to aim for perfection. An ideal job search plan with the bar set too high, almost guarantees failure. This is the time instead to develop a realistic plan of action - small but consistent steps you are reasonably sure you'll be able to complete, day after day. Each step will move you further along while also giving you the satisfaction of checking things off your "to do" list. Having a daily list of doable, tactical items will help you conquer frustration simply by putting yourself in a position to complete those items, one by one, with consistency being the name of the game.

Pair with this tactic an accomplishment log that you complete at the end of every week, where you write down ALL your job search actions taken. Having a realistic plan of daily action combined with an accomplishment log where you record (and acknowledge and celebrate) your results will help redirect from overwhelm and frustration transitioning you from the idea of "perfect" to "done."

Set A Negotiating Target: The offer negotiation can be a stressful and frustrating part of the job search, especially when you aren't being offered what you believe you deserve, whether in salary, equity, benefits, or all of the above. This is why it's important to get clear on day one about what your priorities are and the most important things you want to negotiate around.

Do Your Homework: A common source of frustration in job searching and in life results from a lack of preparation. An individual who does his homework and finds out what he needs to know in advance of a situation, is much less likely to experience the frustration of someone who goes in unprepared. Knowledge and preparation add to your Career EQ power. Don't just "show up" to job situations without putting in the advance work and expect things to magically work out in your favor. It does not work that way, in any industry or in any type of economy.

This also applies to setting realistic expectations. Expecting to make $130,000 right out of college because that's how much other people are making that who have worked in the industry for years is not realistic. You need a track record in order to progress to that level. This is another example of where doing your homework is critical in avoiding needless frustration.

Anxiety

Focus On What You CAN Control: Are there any job search behaviors you're currently engaging in that might be harming your search or at minimum, not helping it? Are you allowing your anxiety to disguise itself as "due diligence" and throwing up disclaimers and apologies to potential employers that are really unnecessary? If you are, but you believe the details are important, consider changing the timing of the information so it's less of a potential barrier in the hiring process.

Practice Networking: If the idea of networking makes you anxious, find a "conversation buddy" to practice networking with. The more you do it and the more people you do it with, the less of an anxiety provoking experience it will be for you. If you're anxious about speaking in general, seek out your local Toastmasters chapter. You'll get practice speaking in public and another tactic the group teaches, is getting comfortable with pauses and silence - a valuable technique in networking and interviewing.

Change Your Language: Review the language of the job search, preferably out loud - laid off, out of work, looking for a job, networking, interviewing, salary negotiation, etc. Are there any words or phrases that make you feel anxious? How could you rephrase them in a way that feels better to you?

Uncover the Root Cause & Reframe: If you're feeling anxious - or simply nervous - about your job search, one initial small but important step you can take is to ask yourself: "What's the root cause of these feelings?" Identify specifically what it is that you're feeling anxious about - Networking? Interviewing? The idea that you might *never* get another job (which is statistically improbable to say the least)? Once you've identified the source of your anxiety, see how you can reframe it from negative to positive.

For instance, if the idea of "networking" is freaking you out, why not call it "reconnecting" with old friends, acquaintances, and other contacts who might be able to help you? If you're feeling anxious that you might "never" find another job, can you find evidence making that real? Has anyone you know ever lost their job and then simply *never* got rehired - ever again? Do you know anyone who initially couldn't find work in their field but when they went and explored other options, they did? Look at the number of available jobs in your industry. How statistically probable is it that you're not a fit for *any* of those jobs?

Name the source of your anxiety, find evidence to support or deny its existence, and, when applicable, reframe it from negative to positive. Or, as author Susan Packard says in her book *"Fully Human: 3 Steps to Grow Your Emotional Fitness in Work, Leadership, and Life"* - "name it, claim it, let it go." In Career EQ, name the source of your job search anxiety, acknowledge that you're feeling it, find the right tactics to deal with it and let it go.

Get Clarity: For some people, the idea of a "job search" is a fuzzy, out-of-focus picture. Lack of clarity on what it actually takes to get a job, especially when compounded with the stress of a recent job loss, can set off anxiety and if there's a potential career change involved, even create a sense of overwhelm.

If this is you, make a list of every single question you have about the job search, all the unknowns - from the largest details ("how long will it take?") to the smallest ("how do I update my LinkedIn profile headline?"). There are no stupid questions and no details too small to address, especially if they will move you out of anxiety and into action. With greater access to information, answers, and resources than ever before, there is absolutely no reason to sit alone in the darkness, suffering from the anxiety of not knowing.

If you have anxiety because you're not clear on your personal brand - who you are, what you offer, and what you want to do - take the time to get answers to these questions as well. Brand clarity means more intentional, specific action steps in your job search. This clarity will also improve how people view you because you'll be seen as articulate, competent, and confident!

Move One Rock: Stare at a mountain of rocks for too long and it will absolutely seem unmovable. Similarly, it might sound like a big task to move from anxiety-induced overwhelm into action, but in reality, it takes only one, initial, often small task to get the ball rolling. Rather than seeing the job search in front of you like a mountain of rocks needing to be moved, focus on moving one single rock in front of you. You could sign up for an online course to sharpen one of your career skills, or you could assign yourself a research assignment about current market salaries in your industry, or you could set a date for completing your resume, rewriting your cover letter, writing your elevator speech, or you could refresh (or set up) your LinkedIn profile. Then move the next rock, and so on.

From a strategic place, and also to get all the anxiety-inducing details out of your head and onto paper, you might make a list of every single rock that needs to be moved and add deadlines to each one. That will become your job search action plan.

This tactic also falls under the category of focusing on things you *do* have control over, which is a huge deal in a typical job search full of unknowns. Taking structured, incremental steps can move you out of anxiety created overwhelm and paralysis, all the way into actual excitement about the job search (as you'll learn more about later in the book)!

Unplug: There was a time not long ago, when the job search was limited to the telephone, mail, fax machine, and then personal computer. If you weren't around any of these forms of communication, you got breaks from the stress and anxiety of the job search. With 24/7 access to smart technology this is no longer the case. Our phones, tablets, laptops, and tech wearables have become so ingrained in our daily lives that sometimes we might not even realize how often we're "checking" them for updates, including responses from employers. Thanks to your smartphone, you can literally get rejected for a job while sitting down to an otherwise pleasant family dinner. With smart technology, breaks from job searching no longer exist unless you make the *conscious* choice to create them.

If you find, especially after reading this chapter, that you are or might be prone to anxiety, I highly recommend creating breaks and "rules" around smart technology. One example of a rule might be to set up a separate email that you use only for your job search. This will be valuable, for instance, if you're checking your regular personal email for a delivery update on that Amazon order you've been waiting for, but with job hunting emails mixed in, you accidentally fall down the rabbit hole of replying to job-related emails for hours on end. Creating a separate email for your job search will help you separate it from the rest of your life - physically and emotionally.

Also consider setting your phone aside - or at least turning the notifications off - for a set number of hours each day to give your mind the opportunity to consciously disconnect from your job search. This allows you to reset all that emotional capital that you'll need for the duration of the job search (which is a marathon, not a sprint). Career EQ means understanding how your emotions work and setting boundaries accordingly for yourself, especially when you find yourself under the influence of potentially detrimental outside factors like technology.

Volunteer: One Career EQ raising tactic for anxiety and really any of the emotions we've been covering, would be to volunteer, even for an hour or two a week. Loss and paralyzing emotions have a way of festering the more you sit and dwell on them. By finding a way to get "outside yourself" and focus on helping others, you're moving your attention away from those emotions and toward making a positive impact on others. Find a way to be of service to others and treat it like any of your other job search tactics.

Loneliness

Seek Positive Feedback: One way to snap out of the spiral of either lack of or no feedback during the job search, is by actively and intentionally seeking positive feedback from others about your value, skills, work experience, and other positive aspects of your brand impression. This is not some artificial ego boost. If seeking objective validation of your value allows you to keep moving forward in your search - then it's a productive, useful job search tool like any other.

Make New Friends: It's beneficial to your long term Career EQ - and overall emotional stability and balance - to create friendships outside of work (and this also means offline!). Look up professional or trade organizations in your area, hobbies or leisure activities that seem appealing, meet-ups, or college courses to bolster your skill set or, just for fun, like ceramics or music appreciation. If you're currently employed, consider a strong social network an emotional buffer in the event that you do lose your job. If you're currently between jobs, use this extra time to branch out, explore some of the activities listed above, and hopefully make new friends in the process!

Job Search Support Groups: If being unemployed feels like being alone on a desert island, a job search support group is the arrival of a cruise ship filled with new friends who can relate to what you're feeling and going through. Preferably, and in the name of combating loneliness with human connection, you can find a local in-person group.

But if you can't find one, finding an online group can also be a good option. If you're feeling isolated in the job search process, and reaching out to friends and family members isn't something you're ready to do, a support group of your fellow job seekers can create a safe "home base." You can share your frustrations, your feelings, and in many cases, networking contacts, tips, and resources with your fellow seekers. Being around other people in the job search will help normalize the situation, help take away any shame or guilt, and give your emotions some space and a chance to breathe before they build up and become potential obstacles.

Take Breaks: When you're between jobs, it can be tempting to see your temporary joblessness as an urgent, time sensitive problem to be solved. This perceived urgency can make a job seeker - especially ambitious or Type A individuals - believe that the only acceptable activity is to look for a job - constantly, during all their waking hours, and without allowing themselves leeway to do anything else. This "all in" mentality can add even more anxiety and stress to the job search and, if exercised over an extended period of time, may even lead to burnout. To keep your emotions in check and stay at the top of your mental game, take breaks. Better yet, schedule your breaks as if you're still working and each break is an important meeting that you absolutely must attend.

As a starting point, think about how you would spend your breaks at work. Maybe you'd use the time to go for a walk with a friend, run errands, or eat at a favorite restaurant. Thinking of your job search as your current job, schedule some of those same activities into your week now and then keep those appointments. Taking regular breaks gives your mind a chance to rest, ultimately making you more productive and focused. Consider also taking longer breaks maybe a couple times a month, and doing volunteer work as a way of taking the focus off yourself and helping others. No matter what kind of breaks you take, the more you go out, the more you'll be around other people, which, even in small doses, will take the edge off feelings of loneliness.

Accountability Partner: Another tactic for fending off loneliness and at the same time contributing to your job search, is to seek out an accountability partner. This person might also be searching for a job or, it could be a trusted, employed friend. You can use your accountability partner as an excuse to take those all-important breaks, get out of the house, and also for more job search specific tactics like mock interviewing, and resume reviews. The accountability partner can also be someone to objectively assess your personal brand and the impression you're making on employers, and make suggestions for improvement.

Momentum Emotions

Self-Compassion

Super Team & Self Care: Exercise self-compassion by leaning on the people who know you best and want you to be happy, healthy, and successful - your super team! Also, try out various self-care activities and find one that you enjoy and can do regularly. Therefore, look at things like proximity, cost, and time investment to ensure you're positioning yourself for self-care success!

Self-Respect: Realize that the definition of self-compassion goes well beyond "self-care." Dr. Kristin Neff has described it as a combination of "mindfulness, common humanity, and self-kindness." It is whatever you personally need to do to stop, be present, acknowledge that you are a valuable, living creature that deserves self-respect and kindness, and then deliver on that acknowledgment.

Watch Your Language: Through your journaling practice, pay attention to the words you're using to describe yourself, your beliefs, and your job search as a whole. Not just the words you write in your journal but also tune your awareness in to how you talk about yourself to other people. Are you beating yourself up? Downplaying your value? Being verbally pessimistic about your odds of getting the job you want? There's a part of your subconscious mind that is processing and recording every single word and then turning those words into beliefs which then translate into actions.

Ask yourself this - if your subconscious mind was a small child, would you still say the same hurtful things that maybe you've been saying about yourself? On top of that, would you then bring that child with you to your next job interview as part of your first impression?

Watching your language also means not minimizing or making light of your situation. Being out of work can be hard, and there's no reason to downplay or deny how you're feeling. Exercising compassion means being present with yourself in the moment, no matter what that moment may be. Telling yourself "I shouldn't be so upset about this" and attempting to minimize your pain will not make those feelings go away. Instead, show yourself-compassion and understanding for the pain you're feeling, just like you would do for a friend in pain. Give yourself the gift of acknowledgment and then healing.

Identify True vs. False Beliefs: Showing yourself kindness starts with uncovering where you are being unkind to yourself. Be willing to investigate the self-beliefs and innermost thoughts that are holding you back and label each one, based on actual evidence - true or false. Some thoughts might even be a mix of the two, with some of it being true and some of it untrue.

For example, let's say you uncover the limiting belief: "No design agency will ever hire me again because I'm not very good at Adobe InDesign." It is most likely not true that you will NEVER be hired again. However, if you honestly feel that you need more training in InDesign, this might be the perfect time to take a course and sharpen your skills. Self-compassion allows you to not beat yourself for not knowing this program better, so you can extract the constructive part of the belief: the need for additional training. It prevents this one limiting belief from festering into what you see as a "skill fail" that ends up defining you in your mind as a lesser job candidate, which can create a sense of anxiety palpable to others, including employers. This practice will help you separate the true parts of your limiting beliefs from the false parts.

Reconnect With Your Personal Brand: Still finding yourself struggling to exercise self-compassion? This is a perfect time to reconnect with your personal brand - who you are at your professional best, outside the context of your prior company and job description. Revisiting personal brand questions like the ones below, will remind you that while you might be between jobs, you still have the same gifts to offer others that you've always had. Reconnecting with your personal brand can spark a boost of self-confidence, it can shore up the (perhaps battered) walls of your identity, and overall, it can remind you why you're awesome. And who can't use that kind of reminder once in a while?

Confidence

Refresh Your Skills: What can you be doing to refresh your skills and knowledge and give yourself a competitive edge in your search? During this time when you're between jobs, what additional certifications, courses and skills could you obtain? In addition to using them to buffer your resume, sharpening your skill set can do the same for your confidence. The self-assurance (and maybe even swagger!) you gain from your newfound skills and certifications will carry through not just on your resume but in your interview and salary negotiation as well.

Practice: Practice might not make perfect but it almost always acts as a confidence builder. As we've talked about in previous chapters - mock/virtual interviewing, networking practice, and even visualization, can help you work out the kinks, while also building emotional muscle memory around the scenario so when you're in the real situation, you'll feel confident in your performance.

Practice also extends outside of interviewing to the salary negotiation, something many job seekers struggle with. Rehearsing potential salary conversations is a big confidence builder. It's worth the extra practice because by that point in the process you've almost crossed the finish line. Why not put in the extra effort, practice negotiating to get paid your value, and finish your job search strong?

Set Physical Cues: Think about a time when you felt confident in your talents, abilities, skills and overall value. What helped you created that emotional state - hitting a certain goal, listening to certain music, holding an object that made you feel confidence, reading a certain passage of a book? Tangible cues like physical objects or totems can trigger your past memories of confidence, bringing them into the present with you. Another example would be, like many professional athletes do, listening to a certain song that boosts your confidence.

Get a Part Time Job: One way to keep your confidence up, while also creating a cushion of income and maintaining a routine and structure in your life (therefore avoiding many of the loss and paralyzing emotions), is to get a part time job while searching for your next career opportunity. A part time job, no matter how seemingly small or insignificant, creates purpose and confidence. On top of that you might discover new skills and talents that you never knew you had, further increasing your confidence. Challenge yourself to seek a side job that stretches you as a person and a professional!

Finish Your Resume: Once a job seeker completes their resume, their confidence really begins to kick in. The task of pulling together past successes and accomplishments holds up a confidence boosting mirror, reminding the individual of their value. Many a job seeker has told their coach after completing their resume, "Wow, I look pretty good - I'd hire me!!"

Focus on the Controllable: The quickest way to drain your self-confidence is by expending energy and worry on things beyond your control. Focusing on rejection, negative feedback, or no feedback at all feeds the little voices in your head of self-doubt - the ones telling you you're not good enough. Starve the voices by shifting your attention only to things within your control - resume, interview practice, even your interview clothes. Wearing clothes that make you feel powerful and attractive is something within your control that is also a huge confidence builder.

Finally, no matter how out of control the job search seems, you always have the opportunity to control your stress. Allowing stress to accumulate will affect your confidence levels. Things like self-care, changing your self-talk, and positive affirmations and self-talk can replace stress with forward motion. All these things can remind you to exercise your power of choice which can take you out of hopelessness and into confidence.

Reconnect with Your Self-Worth: If much of your self-worth was attached to a job you no longer occupy, that blow to your identity can also be a blow to your confidence. Tap into a deeper awareness of who you were outside of that job, the skills, talents, and successes you had before it and additional ones you've gained because of it. What past successes can you draw on to build your confidence now? Losing one job position doesn't take away the value of any of your contributions. Reconnect with all that value, draw confidence from it and use it to zoom out and see your wholeness - the complete and valuable person you are outside of your jobs. What value do you bring to a workplace, your community, and the world?

Apply for a Stretch Position: For bonus confidence building points, stretch outside your comfort zone, find a job that you feel you're not a perfect fit for (but one you really want!) and apply for it. Maybe you have some of the skills and experience required, but not all. Therefore you'll have to somehow convince the hiring manager to give you a shot anyway because you can do the job and learn the required skills. Put your confidence to the test by selling yourself for a position just above your qualifications. What's the worst that could happen? What's the *best* that could happen?

Excitement

Write a Mantra: Think of specific words and messages that trigger excitement in your heart and soul when you read them.

Play around with several options if needed and come up with a message that makes you the most excited when you say it out loud! Then, write down your mantra and keep it in a visible, easily accessible place (for example, an index card taped to your desk or, in a graphic as the background image on your phone or computer) so you can tap into that excitement as needed.

Ask For Feedback: Be willing to ask for feedback and when you do, be specific, which will make it easier for those you ask. First, write a list of all your strengths and positive character traits. Next, ask your friends, industry peers, employees, and coworkers (if applicable) to draw up the same lists about you. Seeing yourself through other people's eyes can provide just the boost of confidence and excitement you need to power your search, no matter what stage!

Face to Face Interaction: No matter how you're feeling, make it a priority to take your job search outside to the light of day and give it some air. Being around other human beings is sometimes just the emotional trigger needed to pull yourself out of the job search doldrums and into excitement about future possibilities. When circumstances keep you from in person interaction, much like safety measures during a pandemic, interpersonal meetings on social media platforms or other technology are just as effective for the purposes of job searches.

In addition to networking, you can also engage with other people by taking part in hobbies, volunteer work, and even branching out your job search strategy to include employer visits to companies you're interested in working at by meeting people that work at those organizations. And you never know when the hiring manager might be feeling generous and agree to meet with you if you happen to be around the corner! Pro Tip: Have a business card and resume on hand just in case the situation should arise.

Practice Gratitude: There are two aspects to this tactic. First, don't get so excited about a potential job that you forget the crucial last step in your job search, the thank you follow up.

The other aspect reframes the purpose of the follow up. After you've been rejected for a job, as a way of processing your temporary grief over the loss and moving back toward excitement, send a follow-up note to the employer thanking them for taking the time to meet with you and telling you about the company, introducing you to other team members, and asking them to please keep you in mind for future opportunities at the company.

This one simple gesture not only helps you move through the emotions around the temporary rejection more quickly, but it also creates forward momentum by taking this next step in your job search.

Balance Excitement with Self-Awareness: Making this tactic work is dependent on the work you've done on your personal brand. You must first have self-awareness of who you are as a person, your gifts, what you have to offer an organization, and your goals. Then, the excitement you exhibit to a potential employer about a job is grounded in authenticity, and therefore not excitement for the sake of excitement.

Focus on Future Opportunities: Perhaps you're finding it challenging to let go of your prior job, stuck in the emotions of having such a "perfect" situation ripped away from you. As long as you're grieving your last job, it will be hard to generate excitement for your next job opportunity. Consider the possibility that you might be looking at your last job through rose colored glasses. Was it really as ideal as you thought it was or are you romanticizing it?

Here's one way to get a more accurate picture. Grab a piece of paper, and draw a line down the middle to create two side-by-side lists. On the left side, write down all the things you liked about your last job, how it aligned with your core values and personal mission, skills and talents it helped you develop, and all the future opportunities it afforded you to grow your career. What's missing from this list that you might possibly be able to find at your next job? Focusing on future career opportunities rather than obsessing about what you've lost, will help you process the grief of losing your last job and generate excitement about what is yet to come!

Appendix B

Super Team Guide

The "Super Team" is a hand-selected job search support team that can include family members, friends, former colleagues and co-workers, or a coach of some sort. In addition to your partner, family, friends, and potentially former colleagues or people that know your industry, also consider adding a "wise counselor" – someone with the capacity to offer deeper meaning and bigger perspectives to events; possibly a spiritual or religious advisor, teacher, or mentor.

Who you ultimately choose and how and when throughout your search that you choose to utilize them, is entirely up to you. I recommend selecting trusted, emotionally available people in your life who are willing to listen empathetically, are willing to be on your Super Team, and will promise to make themselves available for conversations when you need them, and let them know how you see their role in your job search. In other words, don't wait until you reach an emotional crisis in your search and *then* pick up the phone and start venting, catching the person off guard!

This section is specifically written *to* your Super Team, with questions, prompts, and activities from our IMPACT Group coaches that they can use to support you! This is the time to hand over your copy of this book to the people in your life who are rooting for your success and have volunteered their time and support to help you achieve it.

How to be a Helpful Super Team Member

Listen!

Don't feel the need to "fix" their situation, especially at first. The greatest human need is to be heard. Ask the job seeker questions like what's on their mind and how they're doing, and then listen to their responses without passing judgment or trying to fix their situation. Recognize that what they're going through is not easy, emotionally, mentally or physically. Provide a safe, judgment free space where they don't feel pressured to pretend "everything's fine" - where they can feel what they're feeling, express themselves, work through their emotions and when they're ready, take the next step of moving forward. This can be especially helpful for wives of proud men who value their role as "family protector."

Watch Your Language

People generally don't like to be told what to do. Therefore, do your best to avoid black and white language like - "You should do this," or "You need to try that." Rephrases might include, "Here's something I do when I feel like that," or "I've heard that this is a successful strategy." Communicate constructively, understand, and validate.

Offer Accountability

When the individual feels ready, sit down together and write, and agree on an accountability plan. Schedule appointments whether daily, weekly, or monthly, in person, by email, phone, or social media, to check in on the job seeker's progress, and the actions they've taken since your last check-in.

Change the Subject

"How's the job search going? Have you found a job yet?" When someone is between employment, a constant barrage of questions about their job search, even from the most well-meaning people can feel tiring and even defeating. Make it a point of focusing on other things happening in the person's world, personal and professional (perhaps they're taking an online skills certification class). Be a safe refuge from the constant job search talk.

Catch Them Doing Things Well

Recognize something that the individual has done well in their past or present and take the time to mention it. Sometimes in the haze and stress of the job search, they may forget past accomplishments. This also means noticing the small wins in their job search and reminding the person to celebrate! To intentionally prompt a celebration, ask the job seeker to make a list of all their achievements (whether lifetime, short term, long term or recent is up to you and them).

How Can I Show Up Best For You?

Ask, rather than assume that you know what they need. Maybe they just need you to sit quietly with them, or put your arm around them or hug them. Ask, "How can I give you what you need in the way you need it?" It might be check-in texts or emails, accountability checks, help shopping for interview clothes, brainstorming with them about jobs that fit their skill set, proofreading their resume and other documents, or being their mock interview partner including offering feedback on their body language, rate of speech, eye contact, and other aspects of interviewing.

Helping Introverted Job Seekers

Understand that introverts generally will process their emotions internally first before sharing them with another person. Therefore, allow the individual time and space to be alone and quiet to experience and process their emotions. Let them know you're available to talk and provide emotional support whenever they're ready. Offer to connect the job seeker with potential networking contacts via personal email introductions, which will get the conversation rolling while allowing the job seeker to respond how and when they want. You might also set up a coffee date with yourself, the job seeker, and another person you think has connections in their industry or functional area, as a way of taking the social pressure off.

Helping Extroverted Job Seekers

Extroverts tend to process their emotions externally by sharing and talking through them with their family or friends. Therefore, as a member of their Super Team, you can help by being readily available to the job seeker from the get go, to help them talk through and process their emotions. You can also provide the individual with a list of networking contacts and groups, and they are more likely to enthusiastically reach out and engage on their own with little prompting needed.

Distractions

Offer to be a source of distraction! This might mean suggesting breaks and distractions from the stress of the job search with fun activities like weekly coffee, movie, or TV binge watching date. It could also mean volunteering together, as a way of moving the focus away from their struggles and onto others. Or, from the standpoint of self-care and exercising to stay healthy and burn off steam, you might suggest working out or going for walks, runs, or bike rides together. An increase in activity can help process many of the emotions associated with the job search.

Normalizing It

Being between employment might feel isolating, so sometimes it's helpful to remind the individual that they're not alone, and perhaps share a story about a time when you were in their situation. This does not mean to downplay or generalize their specific situation but rather to emphasize that they will get through this - there is a light at the end of the tunnel. Remind them that this situation isn't their fault and they are not being "punished."

Manage Your Own Emotions

It's easy to imagine how a spouse/partner can become emotional about the job search process as well. Maybe you feel like you're picking up an extra emotional load, plus the same chores around the house (or more if you've cut back out outsourcing help for financial purposes), and if you're working, now the financial well being of the family may feel like it's on your shoulders. You adding your own emotions to the mix certainly won't help your partner land a job more quickly, but it's still important to be self-aware of your emotions too.

Rather than giving in to your emotional instincts, first see if your emotional state is a reaction to your partner's. For example, if you're frustrated he's not getting off the couch, then what is the emotional driver for his current state and see how you can help him get to the root cause to solve that block within himself. Or if you're feeling fearful of your financial situation, it's best to get that out in the open, not in a blaming or hysterical way, but to make sure you both are dealing with the facts of your financial circumstances. Do you need to agree to cut back on spending together? Solid communication during this time is key, but make an effort to have additional emotional outlets for your concerns besides your partner to keep them as unburdened as possible.

Have Your OWN Super Team!

Especially for spouses/partners of those in career transition, find a confidante for yourself so you can stay objective, supportive, and to avoid taking things personally. Also, be sure to educate yourself on the emotions of the search by reading everything else in this book!

Emotion Specific Strategies

Anger

Disentangle Your Own Ego

Understand that the job seeker is going through a stressful time and may lash out at you and others at times. Try not to take it personally. Listen and be supportive, removing yourself from the situation as needed.

Ask Questions

Seek to understand how the job seeker deals with stress and frustration. Do they need space? Do they want to talk about it? Do they need reassurance? Try to pinpoint what area of the job search process angers them the most. Is it the aftermath of an interview? Is it networking? Is it resume writing? Perhaps there is a stumbling block that someone else can help the job seeker with. A career coach, a counselor, a peer or even a class or training session might offer some solutions for the job seeker to move past that area.

Set a Timer

If the job seeker seems stuck in 'venting mode' make an agreement that for future conversations there will be 5 minutes for venting and then the rest of the conversation needs to be on actions for moving forward.

Run Errands

Be an extra set of hands! Offer to run errands for them so they can focus on their job search activities.

Fear

Offer Validation

Validate, validate, validate! Do not discount their fears. If you're hearing something that sounds irrational, ask questions about it to help them come to the conclusion on their own that the fear is irrational. Examples of questions could be: "What makes you think that would happen?" "What is the worst case scenario, and how can you plan for it if that should happen? What can you do to keep that from happening?"

Name it & Claim It

Help the individual name their fears out loud. Naming fears can help to release them - or at least begin to assess the rationality of the named fear. Once you and the job seeker have named their fears together, brainstorm potential action steps for overcoming them.

Avoid "All or Nothing" Thinking

Help avoid catastrophic thinking by gently reminding them to take one day at a time.

Be Encouraging But Realistic

Do NOT provide false hope ("oh, you will be fine" "you will get hired in no time") while also offering validation of their job search efforts and encouragement to keep moving forward.

Celebrate!

Help the individual celebrate the little wins. Even the smallest things are big when in a state of fear and job transition.

Network

Go through your respective contact lists and combine your networks, identifying all the possible people that could be of help in their job search. Just seeing that list of potential supporters and resources at the ready, may help calm fears and anxiety.

Past Triumphs

Remind the individual of times when they conquered fear in the past. Encourage them to step out once again and "do it afraid" because you have faith that they can!

Mind-Body Exercises

Encourage the job seeker to try holistic approaches to incorporate into their daily life to help manage the fear/anxiety, which can include: meditation/breathing exercises, yoga/physical exercise, spiritual/faith practices, and dietary changes (including reducing caffeine and sugar intake).

Paralyzing Emotions

Denial

Be Patient.

Willfully ignoring facts about being in transition helps some people keep their wits about them in chaotic situations. They might need more time than others to face the realities of how they ended up in transition.

Calmly Repeat The Facts.

Without sounding judgmental, calmly present the facts. Write them down, if that helps. Repeat. And repeat again, as necessary.

Distinguish Denial From Lack of Knowledge.

Share articles. Encourage conversations with experts, or with others who've been in similar circumstances.

Gentle Encouragement

Encourage the person to talk about the very things being avoided. Gentle questions around the job search can help the person explore what they're running from. Gentle encouragement is based on authentic compliments and helping them to see their strengths from the best possible light. "You can do it," or "you'll get an offer soon!" is not specific enough and might just come across as an empty platitude.

Denial vs. Giving Up

Don't confuse denial with giving up hope. Denial is avoidance. A clear grasp of the factual realities is among the many aspects of a healthy, hopeful perspective. Help the person in transition keep the hope alive every day.

Don't Push

Don't push them at first. Denial is a buffer that initially protects them from often very strong emotions (such as shame, loss of self-identity, self-confidence and purpose, etc.) and allows them to continue functioning. Rather than thrusting the "facts" of the situation in their face, step back and see if the person needs more time to process their emotions first.

Make it "We"

If you need to have a tough talk with the person, schedule a specific time to do it. Don't bring it up unexpectedly. Make it a "we" conversation and refer to the situation as "ours" not "theirs" alone. Without sounding judgmental, calmly present the facts. Then explain that you want to help (with whatever the issue is at hand) – even if it is just a chance to listen and allow them time to reflect.

Reflecting on problems or hiccups in the job search is pivotal to moving through this stage. Don't enable them to stay in a negative thought process.

Frustration

De-Escalate

Neutralize the frustration. When you try to control a frustrated person in a career transition, they may become defensive and more frustrated. The calmer the support person remains, the quicker the frustration may subside.

Be Assertive and Respectful

By being assertive, you empower your partner to take their share of responsibility for how they ended up in transition.

Practice Patience and Compassion

Beneath frustration typically lies deeper and more vulnerable emotions such as fear, sadness, or pain. This is why patience and compassion are key not just through frustration, but throughout the entire emotional process of the job search.

Anxiety

Acknowledge Wins

Ask what the job seeker feels they have done well with their job search and acknowledge and validate each item.

Bite-Sized Chunks

Help them break down the job search into smaller parts so that the whole process does not feel overwhelming (week one, resume; week two, cover letter; week three, LinkedIn).

Controllable Parts

Prompt the job seeker to make a list of the parts of the job search they have control over and the parts they do not. Encourage them to let go of what they do not have control over, and focus on action items where they do have control.

Interview Practice

To alleviate interview anxiety, offer to help them prepare for interviews including practicing mock interviews. Another idea is to watch YouTube videos together, of individuals answering tough interview questions.

Gratitude & Mindfulness

Encourage the job seeker to set daily habits in place like exercise, gratitude journaling, meditation, and other calming practices.

Loneliness

Time Assessment

Ask questions to get a sense of how the job seeker is spending their days and how those activities are making them feel. For example, are they spending 8 hours a day online doing nothing but applying for jobs, leaving them feeling lonely and frustrated? Sometimes simply asking the questions and getting the information out into the open, is enough to prompt a productive conversation leading to changes in behavior.

Getting Out

Find reasons to get the person out of the house and participate in outside activities (small and low risk at first and gradually bigger). Encourage them to re-engage with groups or professional associations they were interested or involved in before their job loss.

Feeling the Love

Encourage the job seeker to make a list of all the people who love them and all the people they love back.

Momentum Emotions

Self-Compassion

Let Them Be Where They Are

To the job seeker, self-compassion is letting them be where they are in the moment without getting stuck, down on themselves, or ruminating in negativity. It's being able to let go of any unproductive thoughts or feelings, letting them pass through like floating feathers. As a member of the person's Super Team you can support this notion by helping them see the bigger picture, the question - "What purpose does it serve to beat yourself up?" "How is it serving you to bang your head against the wall wishing you were in a different place than where you are now?" To continue moving forward productively, it's important for the job seeker to be aware of where they are in each present moment and just acknowledge it. It's okay to be in that spot at that moment in time - it's part of the process.

Compassion

Encourage self-compassion in the job seeker by extending your own compassion to them, through things like listening as they share their feelings and validating their feelings. Also help the job seeker reflect on times when they have had compassion towards others and remind them that they deserve the same compassion.

Ban Negative Self-Talk

Set a rule in place with the job seeker that any negative self-talk is prohibited (and make them commit to the honor system when you're not around). You both might establish something like a "swear jar" where the person has to pay up whenever they get down on themselves and say something negative.

Self-Care

All members of a job seeker's Super Team can encourage the job seeker in extreme self-care (meaning the job seeker makes an extremely strong, DAILY commitment to it): Healthy food, exercise, time in nature, mindfulness practices, relaxation, socialization, and volunteering.

Confidence

Accomplishments

Build up confidence by reminding the job seeker of all they have accomplished, small and large scale. Point out the job seeker's strength and give sincere compliments like, "I think you're being brave right now. I think a lot of people in your shoes might be really frustrated, but you're handling this well." Ask questions like, "What are you doing that makes you feel good about who you are?"

Body Posturing

Research shows that adopting empowered body language, or "power posing" creates the physical and chemical effect of confidence and strength in an individual. An example of "power posing" would be to stand up tall, expand your body to fill the space you're in and with head held high, place your hands on your hips akin to Wonder Woman. Make it a game with the job seeker by doing the poses together!

Excitement

Notice What Excites Them

Make it a point to be observant and reflect back to the individual, where in their life they're showing excitement and encourage them to do more of that activity. This could be going outdoors for a walk, other forms of exercise, reading books by a certain author, listening to certain music or specific songs, watching a favorite TV show, or having conversations with a special person in their life. As a Super Team member, you have the opportunity to be their extra set of eyes, making them aware of a source of potential excitement that they might not have noticed.

You play an important role in your job seeker's search. Recognize that and embrace your role!

Appendix C

Further Reading & Resources

General EQ:

Emotional Intelligence, Daniel Goleman
Fully Human, Susan Packard

Loss Emotions (Grief & Sadness, Anger, Fear)

Hostage at the Table, George Kohlrieser
Do It Scared, Ruth Soukup
No Fear Allowed, Laura Herring

Stagnation Emotions (Denial, Frustration, Anxiety, Loneliness)

Hack Your Anxiety, Alicia Clark
10% Happier, Dan Harris

Momentum Emotions (Self-Compassion, Confidence, Excitement)

Change the Way You See Yourself, Kathryn Cramer & Hank Wasiak
The Gift of Imperfection, Brené Brown
Daring Greatly, Brené Brown
Amy Cuddy: *Your Body Language May Shape Who You Are (ted.com)*

Women in Leadership:

Lean In, Sheryl Sandberg
The Confidence Code, Katty Kay and Claire Shipman
Carla Harris: *How to Find the Person who can Help You Get Ahead at Work (ted.com)*

Networking for Introverts:

Quiet, Susan Cain

Acknowledgements

The book is the culmination of over 30 years of wisdom and experience at IMPACT Group, so thank you to the entire team for helping to pull this book together. Many of our coaches were extremely helpful in crafting the content: Ed Chaffin, Amy Clemente, Dan Coffey, Kelly Cooper-Slayton, Leigh Deusigner, Tami Hollingsworth-Dowd, Jill Forest, Helen Galletly, Nona Haller, Melody Kruzic, Wendy LaBenne, Deborah O'Donnell, Cathy Rogers, and Doug Turner. I couldn't have done it without you! Thank you also to Jennifer Whitten for your input into the Gen Z job seeker. And I couldn't have completed the book without Christine Whitmarsh - thank you for your guidance and partnership in taking this book from its initial conception to a final product.

IMPACT Group clients who have believed in us over the years have also played a big part in us having the ability to write this book. Companies like State Farm, Eaton, Grainger, Walgreens, Pfizer, Boeing, PepsiCo, AT&T, and Amazon, truly care about their people and generously support their employees and their families during career transitions.

I could have never written this book without the inspiration of my mother, Laura Herring. First of all, thank you for starting such an inspirational company, founded on the principles of making a positive difference in people's lives. Your vision and passion inspires me and so many others! I also owe you a huge debt of gratitude for trusting me with your "second child." Thank you for that trust and for giving me the opportunity to also make it my own, too. I would have never embarked on this book journey, though, had I not seen it first hand through the launch of your book, No Fear Allowed! Thanks to my dad, Mike, for your never-ending support of both mom and me, and for keeping us from chasing after shiny objects. I love you both so much!

Finally, to Ted and Kennedy - thank you for being a part of this journey and for your daily inspiration! And to Luca, you are so sweet to share me with this book as we raced to publish it quickly!
  Lauren

About the Author:

Lauren Herring passionately leads IMPACT Group as CEO, where she has transformed the company into a global leader in supporting employees and their families through personal and professional transitions of workforce reductions, corporate relocation and leadership development. Lauren joined IMPACT Group in 2001 and later took over leadership of the company in 2009. Under her leadership, IMPACT Group has helped hundreds of thousands of people find employment.

Take Control of Your Job Search! is Lauren's second book. Her first book, *This Side Up: A Simple Guide to Your Successful Relocation*, supports individuals experiencing the transition of relocation.

Lauren has been awarded the prestigious Game Changer Award by Workforce Magazine and Most Influential Women Award by the St. Louis Business Journal. She also received the Global HR Innovator of the Year Award, presented by GlobalHR Magazine. She is an internationally recognized speaker on the topic of career development and global mobility, has been quoted in the Wall Street Journal and Forbes Magazine, and has published in HR Executive and GlobalHR Magazine, among others. She is fluent in Spanish, and prior to joining IMPACT Group, Lauren worked in economic development in Puerto Rico.

Lauren holds a Master's in Business Administration from Washington University in St. Louis and a Bachelor's in Marketing from the University of Notre Dame. Lauren is on the Board of The Committee of 200, the preeminent global organization for women business leaders. She serves on the executive committee for the St. Louis Regional Chamber, where she is excited to support the economic development of the St. Louis community. She is also on the board of COCA (the Center of Creative Arts), and Connections to Success, where she dedicates her expertise, resources and time to making a difference in her community and others' lives.

Lauren's personal mission statement is to make a positive difference in the lives she touches, and her hope is this book will positively impact each reader's personal and professional life.

Lauren is married to Ted Disabato and is blessed to have his love and support in addition to their two children, Kennedy and Luca.

CPSIA information can be obtained
at www.ICGtesting.com
Printed in the USA
BVHW030200280720
584841BV00001B/100